NEVER ALØNE AGAIN

TO JASON -
WITH MY LOVE -
THERE REALLY IS AN ANSWER
AND A SOLUTION

JOHN FEATHERSTON

ISBN: 1478145552
ISBN 13: 9781478145554

FOR KAY

It might have appeared to go unnoticed—

but I have it all here in my heart

ONE

Saturday, June 3rd, 2006...the night before Pentecost. It felt like my whole life had led up to this moment. A lifetime looking for freedom and the answers. Nearly 20 years of healing and dreaming. 5 months of frantic preparation. The week leading up to this moment spent at the Monastery in the Desert–begging God to bless this new thing–to show up and bring His people. It all came down to this moment, Saturday night, June 3rd...the night before Pentecost.

Those of us that God had called, and brought together, to "birth this baby" had thought about little else these last few weeks. Had we done everything we could do? Was there somebody else we should have talked to? Were all the details in place? We all started showing up hours early. The band went through the music one more time. Jeff was in his little office pacing and mumbling to himself–going over and over the words he'd been preparing for weeks. The welcome crew had the "welcome bags" filled, and the t-shirts folded, lined up and ready.

At around 6:00 we all gathered up in a circle and asked God one more time to bless this new thing. Please, God, send your Spirit tonight like you did that other Pentecost. Bring the people...the broken, the hurting, the lost, the discouraged...please bring them here. Use us to dispense your hope and healing. Do again here, tonight, what you have done for all of us. Please give us this "front row seat" to watch you do what you do.

We were thrilled. We were hopeful. We were anxious. We were ready. Around 6:30 they began to come. First they trickled in...and then they poured in. Motorcycles rumbled into the parking lot. The cars stacked up in the driveway. People who had always believed they didn't belong in a place like this walked through the door to see if it was true. You could see it in their eyes. Is this for real? Do I actually belong here? There was a roar of excitement as the room filled up. People who didn't know each other met. Old friends noisily reunited. Lots of hugging. Lots of laughing.

At straight up 7:00 the screens overhead lit up with a digital countdown. 5 minutes to go. The music thumped. The numbers flashing on the screen worked their way down...:05, :04, :03, :02, :01..."WELCOME TO SERENITY CHURCH!!" The crowd roared!

God began a whole new thing. None of us would ever be the same. Saturday night, June 3rd...the night before Pentecost.

TWO

October, 1987. I'm standing on a sidewalk on the tough edge of downtown Dallas desperately looking for the address the woman had given me on the phone. All the words you use to describe a neighborhood like this: seedy, gritty, crime-infested (and the more politically correct "transitional") all seemed to line up and describe this spot. A boarded-up gas station. An old auto repair. A dilapidated old church with graffiti sprayed on its stately brick walls. A trickle of homeless people slowly shuffling from nowhere to nowhere.

I'm standing there beside my new Mercedes, in my custom tailored suit, and I can't find the address she gave me. Did I hear her right? Did I write it down right? If so, has it actually come to this? Do I really belong here? I had looked up and down that block for the address the woman had given me. Nobody seemed to know what I was talking about. It was nearly noon. She said "noon". I couldn't leave without finding it. Where else would I go? So, I just stood there and watched.

About that time something started to happen across the street. They came first one at a time–then a steady stream of folks began to arrive and then disappear down a dirt alley between the defunct gas station and a boarded-up store front. It was the craziest grab-bag of humanity you could imagine: downtown yuppies, working people in uniforms and work clothes, homeless people in rags. Finally, at straight-up noon the biggest, toughest looking, Harley biker I had ever seen–a blur of beard, leather, and chains–roared his bike down that same dirt alley and disappeared in a cloud of dust.

I had no idea what was going on back there, it looked seriously dangerous, but it was the only place I hadn't looked. I just couldn't leave here until I found the help that woman had promised. I took a deep breath, crossed the street, and started down that alley. Where the alley ended was a rolled-up garage door. Inside were all those people I had seen make their way down that alley. They were sitting in a circle on metal folding chairs drinking coffee out of styrofoam cups. Most of them were smoking cigarettes. I stuck my head around the corner and said: "Excuse me, does anybody know where 4615 is?" Several of them looked over and smiled. One of the guys said: "You found it–welcome home!" He hopped up, walked over to the door, introduced himself, and grabbed me in a big bear hug. He told me to come have a seat in the circle...pointed to a coffee pot in the corner...and said: "Help yourself–we just made a fresh pot." I got a cup of the coffee, found an empty folding chair, and a half dozen more folks introduced themselves to me and all seemed to insist on hugging me.

One of the guys passed out some laminated cards to several of the people sitting in the circle. He said: "Welcome, everybody, to the Thursday noon meeting. Let's have a moment of silence for those we love who are still suffering–followed by the Serenity Prayer." Everybody bowed their heads. For the next few moments you could have heard a pin drop. He took a deep breath and said: "God..." Everybody chimed back in unison: "Grant me the serenity to accept the things I cannot change–courage to change the things I can–and wisdom to know the difference."

Everybody looked up, and one by one he called the names of the people holding the laminated cards and asked them to read what was on them. In the weeks ahead I would know every word they read by heart. That day it was just a blur. When they finished, they all passed the cards back to the man leading the meeting. He looked around the circle and said: "Does anybody have anything they'd like to share with us?"

The first one to speak up was a girl sitting on the other side of the circle from me. She was probably in her late 20s. The first thing I noticed is that she appeared to have some profound birth defects. The parts of her body hadn't formed right. Her arms and legs seemed withered and weren't the same length. When she spoke her speech was slurred, and I had to listen very carefully to understand what she was saying.

"I was born like this", she said, "my body has always been like this. When I was growing up, I just knew that no man would ever find this attractive. I remember when I was a teen-ager at slumber parties with my friends. They'd be giggling and gossiping about their boyfriends—and the boys they wished were their boyfriends—and I just learned to tune all of that out. I just couldn't let my head, or my heart, go there. I knew it would never apply to me.

"Not long ago a man came into my life and we became really good friends. One night we were visiting and he told me he thought I was pretty. I was absolutely flabbergasted. I didn't even have a place to put that. Nobody in my entire life, including my daddy, had ever said they thought I was pretty. Not long after that he told me he thought he loved me. It just seemed like a miracle. Is it possible this could actually happen to ME?!

"Now, he's gone...and I'm pregnant...and I don't expect to ever see him again. The last few days I've hurt in ways that I didn't think were possible. I keep thinking that I desperately need to just not 'feel' for a while. If I could just medicate this pain, if I could just be numb, if I could just not feel for a while, maybe I could handle this better later. Honestly? The only reason I haven't done something that would hurt me, and hurt my baby, is because some of you sitting in this circle have been with me around the clock for the last few days making sure that I don't."

The next one to speak up was sitting just to her left....a very expensive-looking downtown Dallas yuppie. His haircut probably cost more than everything most of those folks were wearing. Beautiful, perfectly fit, custom-tailored suit. Handmade Italian loafers. Rolex watch. A breed that seems to especially thrive in downtown Dallas.

He said: "I love my wife more than my life. That woman is everything to me. You all know that we've really been struggling in our marriage. This week she left me. I came home last night to that empty apartment, and I hurt in ways that I didn't know I was capable of hurting. Cocaine nearly killed me–and did major damage to our relationship. That's why I'm here. That's why I found you. Thanks to you and my Higher Power I have several weeks clean and sober–but it might have come too late to save my marriage.

"Last night I was sitting there alone in that apartment and I thought if I could just stop feeling this tonight, if I could just sleep, if I could not hurt like this for 24 hours maybe I could figure out what to do. So, I picked up my phone to call my dope dealer. I know that I dialed his number, at least I thought I did, but somehow instead I called Bob."

He pointed to his left to that big, scary-looking, biker that I'd seen roar down that alley on his Harley. I immediately tried to piece together what on earth was the connection between the yuppie and Bob?!

He said: "Bob was at my house within minutes of getting my call and sat on my couch with me all night long. We prayed together. We cried together. We talked through it together...all night until the sun came up. Then Bob and I went and got some breakfast and went to work. I guess I didn't start dying again last night because God and Bob wouldn't let me."

Suddenly, I understood Bob and the yuppie. This was something I'd been looking for my whole life and hadn't even known how to ask for. I was born on a Sunday and was in church the next Sunday. I had been taught and trained at two Christian universities and a seminary. I was 34 years old and the Sr. Pastor for one of the largest churches of my denomination in the world. I was witnessing "church" for the first time in my life. These were the people who would save my life, re-write my theology, and change me forever. My life was about to turn upside down and go to places I could not have imagined.

THREE

My name is John and I'm a drug addict and an alcoholic. How many thousands of times have I spoken those words to how many tens of thousands of people? It's all true–but there's so much more that I am. I'm a husband who has been deeply in love with an amazing woman for over 35 years. I'm a dad to a grown daughter and son who are the best people I know. I'm "Papa" to their kids. I've spent my whole life as a preacher's kid...and then a preacher.... in mission fields from Africa to the Caribbean.

I first stood in a pulpit to deliver a message at age 3. We lived in the typical little white frame "parsonage" next door to the country church where my dad served his first ministry as a full-time pastor. I walked into his study one day and asked him what he was doing. He said: "I'm writing my sermon for Sunday." I told him I wanted to be a preacher, too. He said: "Then you have to do what I'm doing." He pulled a piece of paper out of the little notebook where he kept his sermon notes and handed it to me. I sat down on the floor by his desk with my crayons and worked hard on that sermon. I'd think a while and then scribble with my crayon for a while. I'd get out a different crayon, think, and scribble some more. After this went on for a while, I decided I was ready and told him so. "Now, what do I do?" "Well, you have to preach it."

We walked into the sanctuary. He got a folding chair and stood me up on it behind the pulpit. He sat down in a pew, front-and-center, and told me he was ready when I was. I was ready. Obviously, I don't have a clue what I said that day–but he always said I "let him have it"! Apparently, I "preached" that day. When I was done he walked up to the pulpit, picked up the crayon scribbles that were my "sermon notes", and clipped it back into his notebook. He gave it back to me on my 12th birthday. He had it matted and framed with the words lettered across the bottom: "I must be about my Father's business". Those framed crayon scribbles still hang on the wall of my study today.

Coming from a long line of preachers, I knew how hard that life is. It was always just assumed that I'd go into the "family business". For my birthdays or Christmas my grandfather would give me a leather New Testament, or a concordance, or a commentary. Just what every 9 year-old wants for his birthday: a commentary on Paul's Epistles. He'd always say: "Johnny, this will help you when you start preaching." I idolized that man. I never talked back to him–except during those times. I'd say: "Grandaddy, I love you, but that's a terrible way to live. I think I'd rather dig ditches or clean sewers than do that for a living." He'd just smile and say: "Of course you will–I'm praying about it." I should have known that it was over for me. When God and Max T. Neel conspired on something, you might as well give in.

We moved a lot in my childhood. My dad was what I describe as a "gypsy preacher". He was always restless for the next adventure. That meant I was always the new kid in school. Usually, every move was something dramatically different than the place we had been living. I'd have to completely reinvent myself every time. I got good at it. I became a chameleon who could walk into a situation, read people, figure out what it took to fit in that situation, and then "become" that. About the time I'd start to feel like I belonged–the next adventure would appear, and we'd move someplace far away and the process would start over.

My Sophomore year in High School. I was in my second High School...and there was still another one yet to come. A buddy from our church invited me to a camp-out after the football game on Friday night. A dozen of us went to the back pasture of his folk's farm, and a pick-up pulled in with ice chests full of malt liquors. My first time to ever taste alcohol. It was like coming home. Nastiest tasting stuff I'd ever put in my mouth—but by the third one or so it wasn't so bad. I knocked back 14 cans of malt liquor that night. The result was exactly what you'd expect. I dropped to the ground and began to puke my guts up. I basically spent that night face down in the dirt and cow poop in an East Texas pasture trying to vomit from an empty stomach.

When the sun finally came up I crawled up off the ground, splitting headache, queasy stomach, covered with pasture muck, and my first thought was: "Cool! I need to get me some more of that!"

FOUR

College. Ah...college! It was the first time in my life that I knew for sure I'd actually have 4 continuous years at the same place with the same people. My choices were very limited to say the least. My folks said that I could go to any college I chose—but if I went to one of our denomination's colleges they'd pay for it. That excluded their Alma Mater because it had become too "liberal". That left one other option in the state...so there I went.

I walked onto that campus as a man with a mission. Moving into radically different cultures and settings every couple of years of my growing up I had never had the opportunity to "be somebody". I would just have enough time to figure out how to fit and belong in that setting...and I'd have to start that all over somewhere else. Now was my chance. Four years, in one place, with people who were just as new to that setting as I was.

I had the advantage of my "chameleon" skills. I walked on to campus, quickly read how to play the game that fit, and got about the business of playing it. Over the next four years, I became "somebody". President of my class. President of my fraternity. President of the student body.

That's also where I perfected the art of the double-life. I was playing the part beautifully of the student leader at a very conservative fundamentalist Christian college...and black-out drinking and smoking pot with a very discreet circle of friends like me. If any whisper of any of that had reached the wrong people, my academic career would have come to a screeching halt. But, by this time, I had perfected the art of just showing you what you wanted to see.

A recurring touchstone in my faith through those years were my summers. My summer job each year was working as a counselor in our denomination's youth camp in the mountains of New Mexico. I was responsible for a cabin full of adolescent boys pretty much 24/7 all summer. It was also an opportunity to move completely out of myself for a couple of months at a time, reconnect with God, and just have "one John" to juggle.

The Spring before graduation I was wrapping up a degree in Education (anything but ministry). I was doing my student teaching all day...drinking, smoking dope, and partying all night. One night I stumbled into the house I was sharing with several of my fraternity brothers in the wee hours of the morning. My room mate, Ed, was sitting on the couch waiting for me to finally show up. He got up, walked over to me, grabbed my arm and sat me on the couch.

He stood there in front of me in tears and said: "John, I can't do this anymore. I can't just sit here and watch you flush your life down the toilet. You have as much potential to do great things for God as anybody I know, and you're wasting all of it."

For the next several hours God, Ed, and I wrestled for my soul. As the sun came up, Ed put his arms around me and prayed that God would salvage and use all of the things He had poured into me. It was one of those moments that forever changed the direction of my life.

Later that day, I called the director of the youth camp and asked if I could come back that summer. As I got ready to head back to the mountains of New Mexico, I made all the arrangements to start my "real life" when I got back at the end of the summer. I knew what I wanted. I wanted to come back to my college friends, live in that house with my club brothers, and teach school nearby. I applied at every school district in the area, gave them my contact information at the camp, and prepared for a summer of fielding job offers from school districts desperate to hire me. I had a freshly-minted degree in Elementary Education. Men were unheard of in that field. My professors had all assured me there would be an incredible demand for me!

The summer was wonderful. I poured myself into those kids and didn't have time to think much about me. It did begin to dawn on me, though, as the summer progressed...that none of those school districts that I assumed would be so frantic to have me were tracking me down. By late July I had heard from NO ONE and was beginning to panic.

As I mentioned, we were with kids pretty much around the clock. The only free time we had were 2 hours each morning when the kids were in Bible classes. One morning, two weeks before our summer wrapped up, I walked up the hill behind the cabins. I sat on a rock ledge, with a panoramic view of the mountains around me, and did some frantic praying.

I said: "God, if you don't want me to teach school I can live with that–but I do need some kind of answer here! If you're closing that door, please show me the door you want to open for me. Father, you know I'm not subtle. I don't pick up very well on hints, suggestions, and innuendo. Please don't just open the right door...make it crystal clear. Hit me with it, scream it at me, and I promise to do what you have in mind for me...but I need to hear from you!"

The lesson here? Be careful what you ask for! It's a long story that I'll be happy to share with you sometime—but over the next 48 hours leaders from 5 different churches associated with the camp tracked me down, pulled me aside, and asked me to consider serving on their church staffs.

Oh, no! Please, God, not THAT! When the summer wound to a close, and it was time to go back and face life, I knew I had a tough decision to make. I was not happy about it. After desperately praying for a way out of this and seeking the counsel of people I trusted, I chose one of those 5 offers and accepted a position as the Youth Minister for a church in a small college town in the Panhandle of West Texas.

The trip back to load up my stuff, and tell my college friends goodbye, was more painful than I can say. The morning that I was packing my car my buddies were all either in class or at work. I was taking pictures off the wall, loading boxes, and generally pouting and feeling really sorry for myself. As I was walking toward the door with an armload of my stuff, the phone rang and I picked it up.

"Is this John Featherston?"… "Yes, ma'am it is"… "Well, I'm calling from the School District Superintendent's office. We've been trying to track you down. Have you committed to a teaching position yet?"… "No, ma'am, I haven't"… "We have a position open that we'd like to offer you. If you're still interested could you come by our offices and sign the contract I have here on my desk?"… "Yes, ma'am, I'm on my way!"

What, God?! What is this all about? I waited and waited for exactly this job in exactly this place. I finally gave up and did what you told me to do and now everything I've wanted has dropped in my lap. What?!

Then I made the "mistake" of picking the phone back up and calling my dad with exactly those questions. He listened patiently. When I got through spewing my confusion, he said: "It's really pretty simple. God has been relentlessly trying to point you in the direction He wants you to go. You finally sat there on the side of that mountain and told Him you'd do whatever He wanted if He'd just make it unmistakably clear to you. Within hours, He buried you under an avalanche of job offers in the direction of HIS choosing and you've done nothing but whine, gripe and feel sorry for yourself ever since. So, He just gave you the most attractive possible option of YOUR choosing. Now, if you follow His lead it's because you want to—not because He left you no choice."

I hung up the phone, called that nice lady back, and cancelled my appointment. With my car loaded, I drove out of town to the adventure He had chosen for me. For the next several years, I left the drinking and the dope behind and just focused like a laser beam on where this was all headed, starting a life and a family, building a career, and careening into my future.

FIVE

The church that God led me to was relentlessly encouraging to a young guy without a clue what he was doing. Most importantly, they gave me regular opportunities to preach.

I've been asked countless times through the years: "How do you know if you've been called to preach? How do you recognize a Spirit gift?" My answer is always the same: "If you can avoid it...DO! It's an incredibly tough life that God only intends for those that have to do it to be whole."

I knew as I stood in front of those sweet folks and felt Him come out of my mouth that I had no choice. This was a call from God. If He calls you, there is no choice but to follow.

That following Christmas I got a Christmas card from Kay. She had been part of my life all through our college years. I was always fascinated by her. She was one of the most real people I had ever known. She had flaming red hair and eyes that lit up a room. I always felt at home when she was nearby. My pieces fit. I was more "whole" around her. We had dated on-and-off through college and had always been true friends.

Her folks lived just 30 minutes or so from where I was now living. Why don't you drive down for supper some night during the holidays, her card said, let's catch up with each other. I immediately picked up the phone and scheduled a night to come down, enjoy some of her mama's justifiably legendary cooking, and catch up with my special friend.

After supper we excused ourselves to ride around and look at Christmas lights. We rode for hours. By the time I dropped her back at her folks house, in the wee hours of the morning, it was crystal clear to me that this "friend" was something a whole lot more than just "special".

When she went back to start her Spring Semester as a math teacher, I started making at least 2 trips a week (212 miles round trip) to see her. The end of January I took her a ring and asked her to marry me. To my honest amazement she immediately said yes. We set a date for the first weekend after her school year was over and she could move the 106 miles to be with me. On June 4, we stood in front of her home church and my dad performed our ceremony.

We spent the next several years in a frenzy of starting our lives. Shortly after we married, I was called to pastor a church in the suburbs of Chicago. We all but starved during those years, but that little church loved us relentlessly, encouraged us profoundly, and I was able to attend seminary in night classes.

Our little girl was born there. We named her Jenna after 8 centuries of women in my family. When I first picked her up on that Friday evening she was born and looked into those enormous brown eyes, my whole world was rocked. A whole new kind of love exploded in me that day. She's been pretty much rocking my world ever since!

When we wrapped up our time there, we came back home to Texas and I served two suburban churches in fairly rapid succession. Three years after God gave us Jenna, he gave us Jay. Named for both his mom and his dad. He unfolded in our lives as one of the sweetest, most tender-hearted, little boys I've ever known. He has grown up into the best man I know.

SIX

As my preaching/pastoring career began to grow and deepen, I was trying to understand what my purpose was. God had obviously called me–but to what? I began to really struggle with some of the core doctrines and philosophy of the denomination I had grown up in. I loved those people then...and I love them now. They taught me to love Christ. They instilled deeply in me a profound respect and reverence for Scripture. But there was also an oppressive legalism that I couldn't reconcile.

There was very little doctrine or teaching on the principle of completely undeserved "grace". Rightness with God was mostly rooted in procedural correctness. Therefore if your "procedures" didn't match ours, you must me wrong and, therefore, not my brother.

The indwelling Spirit of God was not a miracle working, gift giving, actual presence in our lives. In fact, the age of "miracles" was long over. Miracles stopped when the Apostles died. His influence was limited now to written instructions. The Holy Spirit to us was a retired author. He wrote an excellent book of instructions, dropped it in our laps, and told us to read it thoroughly...understand it completely...and follow it meticulously.

God would meet us on the other side, tally up how well we followed those instructions, and may or may not zap us in the end. We were never sure if we'd make it or not. We wouldn't know until we stood in front of a disappointed God, and He made his final decision. If you asked us: "are you saved?" we would never answer "yes". We'd tell you "I hope so" or "I'm trying" or "we'll see at the end". All we knew for sure was that anyone with a different view of how God works than ours was lost for sure.

From my childhood, none of that made sense to me. I remember missionaries coming to our church to report on their work. They'd tell us that they were the first of "our brotherhood" to take Christ to that nation. As a result of their work, there were now "23 Christians" in that country. Really? People had been preaching Christ for centuries in that place, but He was waiting for us to show up to actually save anyone there?

I had spent hours a week, all of my life, receiving spiritual instruction...and yet I was a college Sophomore before I heard my first lesson taught on salvation as a free gift of God's grace. You can imagine how shocked I was to hear the Apostle Paul say:

"But because of His great love for us, God, who is rich in mercy, made us alive in Christ even when we were dead in transgressions–it is by grace you have been saved. And God raised us up with Christ and seated us with Him in the heavenly realms in Christ Jesus, in order that in the coming ages He might show the incomparable riches of His grace, expressed in His kindness to us in Christ Jesus. For it is by grace you have been saved, through faith–and this is not from yourselves, it is the gift of God–not by works, so that no one can boast..." (Ephesians 2:4-9, NIV)

Really? "Rich in mercy"? "By grace you have been saved"? "Not by works"? What is mercy? What is grace? I began to frantically try to make sense out of huge pieces of Scripture that were completely foreign to me. The answers were shocking. As it turned out, "grace" is God giving us what we don't deserve. "Mercy" is His NOT giving us what we DO deserve. But what about my being right with Him because of my "procedural correctness"? "It is the gift of God—not by works" seemed pretty blunt and self-explanatory.

Suddenly, huge pieces of how I had seen God and approached my faith no longer made sense. So, what was I going to do with that? As I moved through my 20s, two distinct directions for me seemed clear. As I look back with decades of perspective, each one of them was profoundly arrogant. God must have cringed.

First of all, I was going to lead "my people" out of bondage and into the light. Surely they'd listen to me. I was "one of them". Both sides of my family were rooted in preachers and church leaders in that tradition for almost 200 years. I spoke the language. I knew the culture. I would always turn back to Philippians 3 and Paul presenting his Jewish credentials to those Jewish Christians. "I was circumcised on the 8th day", he told them, "of the people of Israel, of the tribe of Benjamin, a Hebrew of Hebrews." His point? I'm one of you. I'm part of the Family. So, listen to me!

That was my story with the people I come from. I knew how they thought, why they thought it, and how they expressed it. Surely, God was calling me to lead them out of legalistic bondage and into the light of this grace, mercy, and the miraculous filling of His Spirit that He had shown me.

That led to the follow-up arrogance that was even more deadly. One night after we had moved back to Texas, Kay and I were sitting in the swing on our front porch. I was pastoring a church in the German Hill Country and we had bought a beautifully restored old cottage near downtown. As we sat there on a warm summer night, I told her that I thought I knew what God wanted me to do. He was calling me to rescue our people from bondage. If I was going to make a real difference, I needed my voice to be heard. For that to happen, I needed to pastor one of our large, important, influential churches. I rattled off a list of 10 of those churches and told her that I intended to be in one of those pulpits by my 40th birthday.

Shortly after my 31st birthday the call came from one of those churches. A huge church offering a huge salary and an influence around the world. They had 9 full-time ministers and the next youngest one was the youth minister who was exactly 10 years older than me. I was the Sr. Pastor with the big office and the breath-taking pulpit in the lavish new facilities they had just moved into on the Interstate. Yep, I had arrived.

It very nearly killed me.

SEVEN

The next few years are hard to remember. A decade or so after we left that place, and that chapter was a distant blur in our rear-view mirrors, Kay and I went back for the funeral of a precious friend who had loved us deep during our darkest hours. After the service we walked those halls and stood in that sanctuary. We both agreed that it was hard to remember ever being there. Maybe that's a gift from God. Maybe it's some form of post-traumatic-stress thing. Whatever, great pieces of those years are sort of a foggy blur to me. That's a good thing.

As so often happens, the achieving of my "dream" was a nightmare for us. That was a deeply troubled church, going through painful transitions, that were really common in our denomination. As we say in the recovery community: "It's not my job to take their inventory." I was in way over my head and out of my depth. I was young, inexperienced, and desperately trying to shepherd a politically charged mega-church through really troubled waters. It nearly drowned me.

By 1986, I was emotionally exhausted, 60 pounds over-weight, and rarely able to sleep though the night. I had a lot of dental work done over several months that year and the dentist would send me home with large bottles of pain killers. A lot more than was necessary to deal with my dental pain. I found out quickly that those pills could cover up more than just dental pain. They could help me not feel. I was really tired of what I was feeling. Best of all, I'd pop a couple of those late at night and sleep, really sleep, for the first time in a long time.

I've always had a pattern of lying in bed at night and worrying till the wee hours of the morning. A couple of those pills and I just didn't care enough to worry all night. It never dawned on me to let anybody, and specifically my God, handle it for me. I had to fix all of those messes. By the time the dental work was done, I found another doctor and another dentist. Finally, they ran out of patience and reasons to prescribe narcotics for me—but I hadn't run out of reasons to want to be numb.

About that time I got a call from an old college buddy who had just moved to the area. He suggested we meet for dinner and catch up with each other. After we ordered he looked across the table at me and: "No offense, John, but you look like crap!" He was right. I did. I was fat, drained, and tired to the bone. I told him that the big problem with me was that I had too much to handle, too little of me to handle it with, and I hadn't had a decent night's sleep in way too long.

He said: "That reminds me of our school days—too many balls in the air and you don't dare drop any of them. You remember how we'd finally wind down? We'd kick back, put on some good music, load up that little pipe, and a couple of hits later it all kinda melted away. I've got a buddy here in the area that I buy a bag from once in a while. You want me pick you up some, too?"

I told him thanks, but no thanks. I'm a big boy now and left that behind a long time ago. But over the next couple of days I began to think about that. Isn't the ability to justify things an amazing process? I've really studied that over the years since. Good people do bad things, smart people do stupid things, all the time. For that to happen, we have to line it all up in our heads where it makes sense. That bad thing really isn't "bad". That stupid thing really isn't so "stupid". I've always been especially good at these mental/moral gymnastics.

So, I made it make sense. Just a little bit, a hit or two, at the end of a tough day and I could wind down, decompress, and stop worrying for a while. If I could stop worrying, I could get a good night's sleep. If I could sleep, I'd be so much better the next day for all of those people who need me. I lined up the excuses all in a row like dominos. Sure, all of that made perfect sense. A few days later I called my buddy back and asked him to pick me up a bag. Just a little bag—because, of course, I wasn't going to abuse it. I just needed a little bit to help me relax.

It worked like a charm. I'd sneak out in the back yard late in the evening, fire up that little pipe, and all the fretting just melted away. There was the inconvenience of the fact that Kay wouldn't tolerate this nonsense—but that was easy enough to solve. I started smoking a cigar on the back porch every night. When she smelled smoke on me she'd assume that's what she was smelling. She just didn't understand. She'd see a problem where there wasn't one. I wasn't going to abuse this. Just a hit or two at the end of the day. It'd help me unwind. I'd be so much better.

Within a matter of days, the line of excuses that I had stacked up like dominos to make this alright...became a lot longer. If it made sense that a couple of hits on that little pipe made bed time better—wouldn't it be nice to be mellow all evening? Instead of just at 11:00—how about starting at 10:00 or 9:00? Dinner was always so much tastier high. How about starting at 7:00 or 6:00? Wouldn't I be better for my family all mellow and relaxed? Why don't I just load up the pipe in the morning, put it in my glove compartment, stop somewhere on the way home, fire it up and come home "happy"? Buying through my buddy became inconvenient so I connected with "his people"...and they had other happy things to change how I feel. Within weeks my late-night-decompressor was taking over my life.

One night I called the guy I bought my dope from and told him I needed a bag. I wasn't prepared for his answer. "Oh, I'm sorry, John, I just sold my last bag. I should have more in next week." Next WEEK?! Nobody is looking for dope next week! I told him that just wouldn't do. I really needed some NOW. He said, "Well, I've got some other stuff here. Will anything else do?" Without even pausing to think I said, "sure". The conversation went something like this: "Well, what do you want?...I don't care...Do you want something to take you 'up' or take you 'down'?...I don't care. I don't care if it takes me up or takes me down. I don't care if it makes me feel better or makes me feel worse. I just don't want to feel THIS!"

Several months into this spiral, I was scheduled to go with one of my oldest friends to a conference in Chicago. I didn't try to hide any of this from him. We had known each other too long and too well for him to "judge me". Every day we'd go to the conference all day and then the minute we walked back in the hotel room, I'd drop my stuff on the bed, reach in my suitcase, and pull out that pipe. He watched this for a couple of days and then finally said: "John, I'm not judging you. We know too much about each other for me to start that. I'm just wondering, is it possible you could NOT do that?"

I was absolutely furious! "I hope you're not trying to insinuate that I'm addicted to this", I snapped back, "any fool knows that this isn't addictive. I don't have to have this. I choose to. It helps me."

He threw his hands up and said: "Alright, alright, whatever you say. If that's true, then try something for me. Put the pipe back in your suitcase, and if it's not a problem for you tonight then pull it back out tomorrow, and I promise I won't say a word."

Then I kicked in with a classic addict response. I snapped back: "I don't have anything to prove to you. I can stop or start doing this anytime I choose. I'm not going to play childish games with you about it." The whole time I'm talking I'm frantically loading and firing up my little pipe.

When we got home, I decided to prove to myself how foolishly wrong he was to worry about this. I'd go a night without it and it would obviously be no problem. So, I went through the evening and couldn't think about anything else. I watched a couple of hours of TV and minutes later I had no clue what I had been watching. Finally, I decided to just go to bed. There was no way I was going to sleep. In the wee hours of the morning, I finally crawled out of bed, sat out on the back patio, and fired up my pipe. The next night I tried it again...and the next...and the next...but I no longer owned this. It owned me.

EIGHT

By October of 1987, I had completely lost control and my life was no longer my own. I was stumbling through the day pumping chemicals into me. Whatever was available. Whatever would help me not "feel". To be able to live with myself in the middle of all of this I had to keep convincing myself that this was helpful. It made me better for my family and the people in my life. If I could sleep, if I could relax, I'd be fresh and alert during the day and available to those who needed me. If I could wind down and be "mellow" at home, then I could be so much more pleasant for my family to be around. A very complicated network of excuses all lined up like dominos. One Thursday morning in October...the lies all died.

I had taken great pride for several years in producing word-for-word transcripts of my sermons each week in advance. We would mass produce them and make them available immediately after I preached them. If you were in our service that day, right before the service ended, the ushers would put large stacks of those transcripts on a table at each exit from the sanctuary. You could pick up a printed copy of everything you had just heard me preach, take it with you, re-study it at home, give copies to friends and loved ones. That way, it wasn't just the people sitting in front of me that received that message—we were multiplying the audience. Soon after we started this we began to receive requests from other places. Not long after that we had a weekly mailing list across the country and around the world.

As you can imagine, this took a lot of work and incredible precision during the week. This was in the '80s. We had pretty much state-of-the-art equipment for the time which was Selectric typewriters, a Dictaphone tape machine, and huge off-set presses in special facilities in our building designed just for the purpose of printing materials to send around the world.

To coordinate all of that looked like this: I would speak exactly what I wanted to say in that sermon into the Dictaphone machine and then give the tape to my assistant. She would type it up on her typewriter and bring it back to me to proof and make any changes. She'd retype it and give it to the woman who ran our print shop. The print crew would shoot metal plates of each page for the offset presses and print large stacks of each page—usually 8-10 pages. They'd bring those stacks back to the office staff to collate, staple and prepare to distribute.

As you can imagine, all of that took some serious precision. A whole team of people were waiting for me to finish my work so that they could do theirs every week. My absolute deadline was noon on Thursday to have mine ready—so everybody would have the time necessary to do theirs.

On an unusually cool, sunny, Thursday morning in early October I got to the office to finish up my studying and sermon prep. I got out my Bible, the books I was using, pen, paper, and Dictaphone equipment. I spread it all out on my desk, looked down, and everything in front of me blurred and seemed to be swimming around in circles on my desk. I sat there foggy and confused, trying to make sense out of all of this, and then the truth hit me like a sledgehammer. I was sitting at my desk with a looming deadline to finish this sermon, with a crew of people waiting for me to finish my work so they could finish theirs, and

I hadn't slept off last night's high. The preacher was sitting in his office completely stoned and couldn't begin to create that sermon.

In one horrible moment, the lies fell down on top of each other. Remember that the way I was able to live with what I was doing was to line up reasons why this was "alright". The first domino in that line was that this would help me to be a better preacher and pastor to these folks. Sitting at my desk stoned...on a deadline Thursday morning, with all of those people waiting outside my door for me to finish my work, and me absolutely incapable of doing that...made that an indisputable lie. If that was a lie, it was probably also a lie that it made me a better husband and daddy. If that was a lie...

In a matter of minutes my whole row of lies fell down on top of each other. I just sat there at my desk and sobbed. What was I going to do? Who could I ask that question? Most people who find themselves at the bottom of a pit can turn to their pastor for answers. I WAS the pastor. Nobody in that church knew anything about what was happening to me. At all costs, I couldn't let them know. So, who? Where? What do I do now?

A few weeks earlier I had been having dinner with a friend. When we finished I invited him to go somewhere with me, I don't remember where, and he said: "No thanks, John, I'll take a raincheck on that. I'm going to head over to a Narcotics Anonymous meeting tonight." I knew absolutely nothing about those people. I had never heard of that organization. I assumed it must be somehow similar to Alcoholics Anonymous...but, then, I didn't really know much about them, either. I assumed this was something to help my buddy with HIS problem. So I said all the appropriate encouraging words and went on about my evening.

Sitting alone at my desk that morning sobbing, shattered, and confused, that's all I could come up with. I remembered that conversation and those people that I assumed were helping my buddy with his problem. I picked up the phone and dialed information. The operator gave me a number for Narcotics Anonymous. I dialed it, a woman answered, and I told her that I believed I might be drug addict. I'm in trouble. What do I do? She gave me an address in the Ft. Worth suburb where I was and told me there would be a meeting there at noon...about an hour from then. "Walk in there", she said, "and tell them what you just told me. They have the answers you're looking for."

I hung up the phone and my next thought was: "I can't do that. I can't walk into a place like that. People in this town know me. What if somebody saw me walk in there? What if a member of my church is in there?!" I picked up the phone and called Dallas information. At least I'd give myself an extra 20 minutes away as a buffer. It was an almost identical conversation. A noon meeting. An address. Be there. They'll help you.

There were no Google maps in 1987. I pulled my big Mapsco book out of my drawer and found that address and how to get there. I walked out of my office and told my assistant that I was sick, I had to go, we wouldn't have a transcript this week.

30 minutes later I'm standing beside my new Mercedes, in my custom-tailored suit, on a sidewalk on the tough edge of downtown Dallas looking for the address that woman had given me. Something started to happen across the street. They came first one at a time—then a steady stream of folks began to arrive and then disappear down a dirt alley between a defunct gas station and a boarded-up store front. It was the craziest grab-bag of humanity you could imagine: downtown yuppies, working

people in uniforms and work clothes, homeless people in rags. Finally, at straight-up noon the biggest, toughest looking, Harley biker I had ever seen—a blur of beard, leather, and chains—roared his bike down that same dirt alley and disappeared in a cloud of dust....

NINE

To understand what was happening down that alley, you have to go back to Brooklyn in the 1930s. Bill Wilson was a wheeler-dealer stock speculator on Wall Street during the crazy boom of the '20s. Like so many high-powered people, he would live at full tilt all day and then use alcohol to come back down. That seemed to work for a while...until Wall Street crashed and there was nothing left but the drinking. Through the early 30s, drinking became Bill's life. He became incapable of earning any kind of a living, and his wife, Lois, fought to keep a roof over their heads working as a department store clerk.

He was in and out of a sanitarium hospital and became the patient of Dr. William Silkworth, who was helping to pioneer an entire new understanding of alcoholism and drug addiction. Addiction was universally considered to be nothing more than a moral failing. If you were a stronger, better person, you could just make a decision to overcome this weakness in your life. Dr. Silkworth had come to believe there was also a primary physical component to the struggle. Some people's body chemistry is just different than other people. For lack of a better description he referred to it as a "physical allergy". The alcoholic's body reacts to alcohol differently than the non-alcoholic. Once this "disease" is triggered, we lose the ability to make rational decisions about when, where, and how much to drink.

This was incredibly encouraging to Bill who had always assumed that the damage he was doing to himself, and everybody he loved, was just rooted in moral weakness. What to do about that, how to change that, was still an unanswered question.

In November 1934, Bill was home alone drinking, as usual, when his oldest childhood friend and favorite drinking buddy showed up at his front door. Bill was startled at his appearance. The last time he had seen Ebby he looked pretty much like Bill... dying of their shared sickness. This was a completely different man. He was clean, shaved, well-dressed and healthy looking.

Bill invited him in, sat him down at the kitchen table, and offered him their favorite drink—gin and pineapple juice. Bill's confusion got a lot deeper when Ebby declined and told him that he was no longer drinking. In fact, he hadn't had a drink in several weeks and didn't want one. How was that possible? Ebby told him that he had found "religion". Bill was horrified. Religion was no friend to drunks. It was "religion" that told him he was just weak and immoral. All of his praying and desperate promises to God had done nothing to pull him out of this pit he was in. He had even written his vow to stop drinking in the family Bible. That had gotten him nowhere. He thanked Ebby for dropping by, wished him luck, but told him he had no interest in "religion". Ebby went on to explain that this was something different. While "drying out" at a local rescue mission, he had gotten involved with a new spiritual movement called the Oxford Groups.

Founded in England by an American pastor, the Oxford Groups believed that there was a systematic way to walk through a relationship with God and be whole. It all centered on what they called "The Five Cs": Confidence, Confession, Conviction, Conversion, Continuance.

"Confidence" is the root of what would come to be called "anonymity". It's believing you can trust the people around you with whatever piece of yourself you share with them. "Confession" meant taking the lid off of all the secrets and hidden things and admitting them to each other. "Conviction" was coming to a willingness to correct the wrongs that were discovered there. This would lead to "Conversion" – a decision of the will to live God's way. What really marked the Oxford movement, though, was "Continuance"...the ongoing, constant, daily support of people who had decided to change.

This would all lead you to become a "free person"–spiritually reborn. To experience this "rebirth", the Oxford Groups advocated four practices: 1) The sharing of our sins and temptations with another Christian life given to God. 2) Surrender our life past, present and future, into God's keeping and direction. 3) Restitution to all whom we have wronged directly or indirectly. 4) Listening for God's guidance, and carrying it out.

Again, Bill told Ebby he was proud for him but had no confidence that this religious thing would do him any good. Shortly after Ebby's visit, Bill was admitted to the hospital under Dr. Silkworth's care for the 4th and final time. This time, he was desperate enough to surrender. He screamed to God: "I'll do anything! Anything at all! If there be a God, let Him show Himself!" He said that what followed was a literal "bright light experience". The room filled with light, he was overwhelmed with joy, and felt real peace for the first time. When he shared what had happened with Dr. Silkworth, he simply replied: "Something has happened to you I don't understand. But you had better hang on to it." Bill never drank again.

When he checked out of the hospital he immediately looked up Ebby and began attending the Oxford Group meetings with him. The process of spiritually "cleaning house", the genuine fellowship of others who were struggling to overcome, was life changing for him. He tried to share what was happening to him with other drunks but met the same kind of resistance that Ebby had found with him. "Religion" had been no friend to them. They had only found judgment and condemnation from those people in those places. They had asked God to rescue them. What good had it done so far?

Several months sober, Bill was offered an opportunity to prove himself by one of his old employers on Wall Street. There was a business deal being put together in Akron, Ohio. If Bill could pull it together, maybe they'd give him another shot. He left Lois in Brooklyn and headed west to put his new sobriety to the test.

After several weeks of effort, through no fault of his, the "deal" fell apart. The other out-of-town lawyers, speculators and negotiators packed up and left. Bill found himself alone and deeply discouraged at the Mayflower Hotel in downtown Akron. He walked down the long, grand staircase into the lower lobby, turned right, and walked in to the hotel bar. He laid a dollar on the bar and the bartender asked him what he wanted. "Nickels," Bill said, "I need some nickels." Armed with a handful of nickels, he walked back out into the lobby to the pay phone. A phone call cost a nickel in 1935. He had noticed a list of local churches and their phone numbers on an easel beside the phone.

He dropped in his first nickel, dialed the number on the top of the list, and when the pastor answered he started the speech he had rehearsed. He explained that his name was Bill Wilson.

He was from out of town visiting Akron on business. He was also a "drunk" with several months of sobriety. He was having a really bad day and was afraid he just might get drunk tonight. If he could talk to somebody like himself, maybe the two of them could talk each other out of it. Did the pastor have a drunk in his church he could talk to?!

We can only imagine what the pastor thought. What kind of crank call was this, anyway?! He ended the call quickly without offering any help. Bill tried the next number, and the next, and the next. Finally, Bill hit pay dirt with the Rev. Walter Tunk. The pastor had no way of knowing how serious this odd man from Brooklyn was–but he was willing to take the risk. Through Tunk, an introduction was arranged with Dr. Bob Smith. Smith was a local surgeon whose practice was coming rapidly to an end because he couldn't stay sober long enough to be trusted with a scalpel. On Mother's Day 1935, Smith was coerced by his desperate wife, Anne, into meeting the drunk from Brooklyn at the home of a friend, Henrietta Sieberling. He promised to show up at 5:00 and stay for exactly 15 minutes. To make sure he wasn't trapped, he brought along Anne and their 18 year-old son.

Bill and Dr. Bob sat down by Henrietta Sieberling's fire and began to swap "war stories" of the madness of their drinking. One story led to another, and another, and another....until the next thing they knew they looked up and it was 11:00. They sat there for 6 hours and miraculously neither one of them had an urge to drink.

They made arrangements to meet again the next night and the next. A week later, Bill accepted Bob's and Anne's invitation and moved into their guest room upstairs in the little white frame house on the corner at 855 Ardmore Avenue. He sent for

Lois and she joined them for the summer. Everyday the men would head out to sanitariums and gutters and drag drunks back to the house to sober up and try their "new way of life". A few stayed and walked this new walk with them.

Following the path of the Oxford Groups, they began to feverishly dig through Scripture looking for the places where God said: "If you will do these things, I will have access to you to do for you what you cannot do for yourself." They came up with pages of long lists. They combined the repeated principles, held on to the passages that told of their struggle and experiences, and finally came down to a list of 12 steps to take them from hopelessness to recovery, and then to sharing that miracle with others.

What began as a small group of desperate drunks drinking coffee around Dr. Bob's kitchen table is today a world-wide fellowship with millions of members, in over 100,000 groups, in literally every corner of the earth.

In 1953, a small group of drug addicts in Los Angeles was given permission by AA to adapt those steps as their own and began the fellowship of Narcotics Anonymous. Today, NA has over 58,000 groups meeting in 131 countries around the world. Those were the folks who were waiting for me at the end of that dirt alley on that hopeless Thursday in 1987. They are the ones who first taught me how not to die.

As the hopeless of all kinds began to realize that life lived in those 12 principles was the only solution that had consistently proven to work–fellowships began to spring up to address all kinds of compulsions and addictions. Today, Al-Anon (for the loved ones and those "addicted to the alcoholic"), Sex Addicts Anonymous, Overeaters Anonymous, Gamblers Anonymous, and scores of other fellowships are helping people to live and heal from an incredible array of physical and spiritual sicknesses. Since each of these fellowships rigorously protects the anonymity and confidentiality of their members, exact numbers are impossible to come by. There are good estimates that over 20 million people around the world sit in those rooms and circles every week making it the largest spiritual movement of the last century.

TEN

For the next week or so, I drove to Dallas every day at noon to sit with those people at the back of that alley. I'd leave every meeting so encouraged, so committed, to do what they were doing and win this battle. But by the time everybody was asleep in our house, all of that commitment from hours earlier was hard to hold on to. In spite of all the promises I had made to God and myself earlier in the day, I'd drag myself out of bed in the wee hours of the morning and pull that pipe and baggie out of their hiding place. Why didn't I just throw all of that away? You'd have to be a drug addict to understand that I was literally not capable of that.

Two things became clear to me quickly. First, I needed a group of those people who were so encouraging to me nearby where I could get to them easily and often. Next, I needed to sit in those circles late at night when my struggle was the toughest. Noon was not my problem. 10:00 at night was my problem. I did some research and found that one of the largest groups in Texas met just a few blocks from my house. They had meetings every day at noon, 8:00, 10:00, and at midnight on weekends. I need to be there every night...late...when the struggle was the hardest. That meant I would have to do the toughest thing so far. I'd have to come clean with Kay.

She and I have always connected and solved all kinds of problems by walking around the neighborhood at night. That night we started down the street and she was excitedly telling me about something that had happened in her day. When she paused I said: "Honey, there's something I need to tell you and it's going to be really hard to say". I just let the words pour out of me. I told her what I had been doing. I told her how I had hidden it all from her. I told her how I had lied to her, and snuck around behind her back, and deceived her every day for all of these months.

Then I said: "I need you to understand that, although I've trampled all over the honesty and integrity of our marriage, I didn't do it at you. This was not about you. I just knew–that if you knew what I was doing–it would worry you and hurt you. If you were worried and hurt, I'd have to stop. I didn't know how to stop. So, the only way I could figure out how to balance all of this was to lie and deceive you. But it wasn't about you. It wasn't at you. Please understand that."

She just stopped walking in the middle of the street. I felt like my heart stopped at that exact same moment. She turned around, looked straight up at me, and said: "And I need for you to understand this: I love you. I love you when you're good and I love you when you're not. I love you when you please me and I love you when you don't. I love you right now. So, what do I need to do to help you out of this pit you're in?"

She told me sometime later that she was actually greatly relieved that night. My wife is many things. "Stupid" is not one of them. She had known all along that something was badly wrong. There was a wall between us that she couldn't get through. All of that time I had been repeating to myself like a mantra that this was making me a much better husband and father...while my family could only see that they were losing me. She finally decided I must be having an affair. She didn't know how to compete with another woman. This she was ready to battle with me.

I told her that I had found this amazing fellowship of people. They had astounding answers for struggles like mine. When I met with them, I had the encouragement to face this thing. I told her I had been sneaking off to Dallas every day at noon and always left so full of hope. Hours later, in the dark of night, all of that resolve was hard to summon back up. The heart of my problem was late at night. There was a group of those folks, close to our house, who met every night at 10:00. I needed to be there every night for a while. I had no idea how long I would need to do this—but it was the only hope I had found.

She said: "Then it starts tonight." An hour later she was standing at our back door with my car keys in her hand. Every night from that night on we'd get the kids fed, bathed, and in bed...spend a little time together...and then a few minutes before 10:00, I'd head out into the night to fight my battle.

My first meeting with the group that would save my life was pretty overwhelming. It was, at the time, the largest group in Texas. It wasn't unusual for there to be over 100 people in a meeting. We'd all cram into a big room for the opening prayer, readings, and giving of the "key tags"...and then break down into several smaller groups in several rooms for discussion. NA, then and now, marks various increments of recovery time with various colors of key tags. You receive the first one for just having the desire to stay clean and sober for one day. It's the white one. Embossed on the back, in gold letters, it says: "Just For Today". I stood in front of the group that first night and took my "white tag".

I went home so full of hope and committed to win this thing at all cost. I lay in bed for hours that night determined not to use. Finally, not long before dawn, I crawled out of bed, pulled my stash out of its hiding place, and got high so I could finally sleep. The next night I tried again with exactly the same result.

On Wednesday night, after the meeting, I pulled one of the "old-timers" aside and asked him: "There's a sign on the wall there that says 'ONE DAY AT A TIME'. I keep picking up these key tags that say 'Just For Today'. That's not working for me. I can't do a day." He sat me down and said: "Then go home and stay clean for an hour at a time. If that's too much, do 5 minutes at a time. Take however much you can handle—and then do another one of those...and then another...and another".

I was scheduled to fly out the next day to speak at a conference out of state. I wasn't flying back until Saturday. I knew that if I didn't take any dope with me I could at least put together 48 hours. Before I left for the airport, I attended the noon meeting of my new home group and picked up a fresh "desire tag".

Also picking up his white tag at that meeting was Danny (not his real name—unless I specifically have permission, most of the names of living people in groups or meetings have been changed to protect their anonymity). Danny was incredibly sick. He was bone thin from the effect of his drug-of-choice. He was yellow with hepatitis picked up from a dirty needle. He was running out of time to finally get this thing. Danny and I were radically different...and exactly the same.

I flew back home late Saturday with 48 hours clean and sober. When I got home from the 10:00 meeting, I sat down in front of the TV desperately wanting to pull my stash out of its hiding place. Remembering the advice I had been given, I decided that there was no way I could bite this off for an entire hour at a time. Maybe 5 minutes. I clicked over to Saturday Night Live. Steve Martin and Sting were the guests that night. Sitting there on the couch I told myself I wouldn't get high until Steve Martin finished this skit. I won't get high until Sting finishes this song. I focused on the blue digital clock on the VCR. I can make it from 11:25 until 11:30. Now I can do it from 11:30 until 11:35. I finally fell asleep on the couch in front of the TV that night. My 3rd night in a row clean and sober.

I made it through Sunday because I was frantically busy—and then totally exhausted. Day Four. I needed that stash of dope out of my house. I needed to dig it out of its hiding place and flush it down the toilet. I was absolutely incapable of any of that. When I got to the office Monday morning, I took a deep breath and called Kay. "Honey", I said, "I've got dope hidden in the house that needs to be gone. I need you to flush it before I change my mind." I told her where it was. She said she'd take care of it. As I hung up the phone I was incredibly relieved, and totally horrified, by what I'd just done.

My lifeline immediately became those people in my "home group". While I was there, while I was with them, I was safe. Danny and I immediately became "war buddies" in those first weeks. We talked every day. We met in the park in the afternoons and read recovery books and the literature to each other. We prayed together. We cheered for each other. We counted and celebrated each day we added.

One of the greatest moments of my life was the night he and I walked in together and picked up our first milestone key tags together. "Clean and serene for 30 days", it said. I wouldn't have been prouder if they'd handed me the Nobel Prize that night.

The next night I walked in and looked around for Danny. He wasn't in his spot. I asked several of the regulars if they knew where he was. Had anybody heard from him? Finally, one of our buddies said: "Oh, yeah, I saw him this afternoon. He's back out there. He was high as a kite when I saw him".

I was absolutely devastated. How could that happen? We had worked so hard to get this far. We had done it together. He was a rock I leaned on. He had helped to carry me this far!

When it came my turn to share in the meeting that night I said: "I just found out that Danny's back out there using again. I can't let that happen. I won't let that happen. When this meeting is over, I intend to get in my car and drive every street in this city until I find him. I'm going to drag him back in here and we're going to start this thing over with him."

I was about to learn the first deep lesson of life in recovery. When the meeting concluded, I started straight for the door. I was intercepted by Susan. By "intercepted" I mean INTER-CEPTED. She was a big, tough, motorcycle-mama who had lived a lot of tough years on the streets and now had years of black-belt recovery. She had a heart of gold but took no crap from anybody. She reached out, grabbed me by my shirt collar, and slammed me up against the wall. She looked me right in the eye and said: "So, who crawled off the cross and made you Jesus?! The only somebody you have any ability to save is you and it looks to me like you've done a sorry job of that so far. If I was you, I think I'd just go on home now and take care of my own recovery. If Danny wants what we've got, he knows where we are. If he doesn't, there's not a damned thing you can do about that!"

I went home. A couple of days later Danny came dragging back through the door with his tail between his legs and started over. If he hadn't, Susan was absolutely right. No matter how desperately we want it for somebody else—nobody can cause it, will it, or force it, into a life that's not ready to receive it. We carry the message. We can't force feed it.

ELEVEN

The next few weeks were a blur. All of this was new to me. I was learning how to live life a whole new way. They told me that there was a handful of fundamental things that had to become the heart of how I live if I was going to win the battle long-term:

...They told me to "hit my knees" every morning before I started my day. Before I walked away from my bed, get face down on the floor and ask God to keep me clean and sober just this one more day. It was important to kneel before God because we desperately need that humility. We are a strange combination of astounding arrogance and utterly crippled self-worth. We have been our "own solution". Our answers, our solutions, our direction of our lives, is all we'll listen to. In the same breath we know how much damage we have done, how miserably our "solutions" have failed us, and how hopeless our situations have become. That's what got us in this mess in the first place. I've heard it described as: "I'm a worthless piece of crap on the bottom of somebody's shoe—and the whole world revolves around ME!!" At the end of the day, I was told to get back on my knees right before I climb back into bed and thank God for another day of victory.

The Apostle Paul was making new sense to me: "Do not be anxious about anything, but in everything, by prayer and petition, with thanksgiving, present your requests to God. And the peace of God, which transcends all understanding, will guard your hearts and your minds in Christ Jesus." Philippians 4:6-7 (NIV)

...They told me to read something every day that fed my Spirit. I was going to have to completely rewire how I think. The only way to replace what they called "stinkin' thinkin'" was to constantly replace those thoughts with something that brought me closer to God and focused me on the weapons at my disposal in the battle I was fighting.

Hmm, I was beginning to wonder if Paul might not have been the original 12-stepper! "Finally, brothers, whatever is true, whatever is noble, whatever is right, whatever is pure, whatever is lovely, whatever is admirable—if anything is excellent or praiseworthy—think about such things.... and the God of peace will be with you." Philippians 4:8-9 (NIV)

...They told me to find someone on this journey with me whose recovery I admired. Ask him to be my "sponsor". A sponsor is someone further down this road than I am. It's someone who has learned what I don't know yet. His job is to monitor my progress and to show me what to do next. I can only get what he has by doing what he does. He teaches me those things. I become willing to take that direction. That kind of relationship means touching base with him every day. If I feel me slipping, he's the first call I make. He picks me up when I fall and is my cheerleader while I run this race and fight this battle.

It's a principle as old as Scripture: "Brothers, if someone is caught in a sin, you who are spiritual should restore him gently. But watch yourself, or you also may be tempted. Carry each other's burdens, and in this way you will fulfill the law of Christ." Galatians 6:1-2 (NIV)

...They told me to "work the Steps". Wanting this was not enough. Believing it could happen was not enough. It's only by DOING the things that have changed and saved millions of lives that I could expect to receive the same miracle. That meant carefully, methodically, walking through...actually doing...those 12 principles that God had put at the heart of these fellowships and the miracles they were experiencing.

There's only one Scripture that is quoted exactly in the "Big Book" of Alcoholics Anonymous. It's the imperative from James that "faith without works is dead". He said: "What good is it, my brothers, if a man claims to have faith but has no deeds? Can such faith save him?...In the same way, faith by itself, if it is not accompanied by action, is dead. But someone will say, 'You have faith; I have deeds.' Show me your faith without deeds, and I will show you my faith by what I do. You believe that there is one God. Good! Even the demons believe that—and shudder." James 2:14-19 (NIV)

I had a professor in college who said that quote: "You believe that there is one God. Good!"...might be better translated, "So what!" or "Big deal!" Knowing that God "can" does not take the place of my relentlessly, faithfully, doing the work of clearing out a place in me for Him to step in and do what I can't do. "Even the demons believe that—and shudder."

...They told me to do whatever was necessary to meet in a circle of recovery, with people like me, every day for the next 90 days. They called it 90-in-90. As far as I can tell, that's a fundamental commitment that goes back to the very beginning of the 12-step fellowships. It's an accepted truth of what it takes to recover in almost all of the various kinds of recoveries. In the early days, the drunks would sit around in their circles and ask each other: "How long did it take for you to really start feeling different about life and the obsession to start to let go?" It seemed to be pretty universal that 90 days was their common experience. All kinds of serious scientific studies have been done in the years since...and remarkably came up with the same conclusion. It takes us about 90 days of relentlessly feeding our heads with a new way of thinking, and our bodies with a new way of living, for the miracle to start to happen.

Like all of the truth in our fellowships, God has been teaching that very thing to His people for a long time. When I was a kid in Sunday School, our teachers would have us memorize "proof texts". These were verses of Scripture that we could use to back up our church's various doctrines. One of the first ones we memorized was Hebrews 10:25 (in the King James Version). It said: "Not forsaking the assembling of yourselves together as the manner and custom of some is." What did that tell us? That was the proof text for: if-you-skip-church-you'll-burn!

Sadly, we missed the whole point of why "assembling" is so important. If we had just included the verses on either side of it, there's such sweet truth there. In the NIV it says: "And let us consider how we may spur one another on toward love and good deeds. Let us not give up meeting together, as some are in the habit of doing, but let us encourage one another—and all the more as you see the Day approaching." Hebrews 10:24-25 (NIV) There's a wonderful reason to relentlessly be together. It spurs us on to love and doing good. It encourages us.

I've always been fascinated by what happened to that first large group of Christ-followers. In one generation the fire that was lit that day went out to literally every corner of the world. What kept that fire stoked? What kept that flame alive?

"They devoted themselves to the apostles' teaching and to the fellowship, to the breaking of bread and to prayer. Everyone was filled with awe, and many wonders and miraculous signs were done by the apostles. All the believers were together and had everything in common. Selling their possessions and goods, they gave to anyone as he had need. Every day they continued to meet together in the temple courts. They broke bread in their homes and ate together with glad and sincere hearts, praising God and enjoying the favor of all the people. And the Lord added to their number daily those who were being saved." Acts 2:42-47 (NIV)

Somehow, I missed the point that these "suggestions" that I was given were ALL non-negotiable if I expected the miracle to happen for me. It wasn't a buffet line that I could pick and choose from. Most of them I grabbed hold of immediately. I felt immediate relief from "practicing these principles". Praying had always been some part of my life. It wasn't difficult to practice it the way they taught me. The literature of recovery was encouraging and inspirational. I could spend some time there every day. God led me to a wonderful first sponsor who was a relentless encouragement to me—and remains a dear friend to this day. The meetings? I felt safe there. I really liked those people. I had no problem doing that every day.

But "working those steps"? That was something else entirely. That was some intimidating stuff...and, as we'll discuss shortly, Step One was a huge problem for me doctrinally and philosophically. Maybe I'd face that "step work" some other time.

That was a mistake that would come back to bite me hard.

TWELVE

There's no way to overstate how radically different life became overnight. This was a whole new world, with completely different people, and a radically different approach to God than anything I had ever experienced before.

The first thing to hit me was a deep resentment. Every night I'd walk into that smoke-filled warehouse full of drunks and junkies and be loved, encouraged, accepted, supported and introduced to a God who loved me fiercely, miraculously, and unconditionally. I felt absolutely safe there.

Every morning I'd put on my suit and tie and drive to the other side of town to go "do church". I could not have felt less safe there. I was absolutely confident that if those folks actually "knew me" they would discard me. My acceptability there rested deeply on a carefully manicured facade that I could never let slip.

Something was deeply wrong with this picture.

One night in the early weeks of my recovery, I came home from the meeting, sat down with Kay on the couch, and told her: "If God will just pick me up. If He will just lift me out of this pit I'm in—I'd love to take all of that power, and love, and healing that happens in that warehouse...weave it through Christ and what he intended the church to be...put all of that in a blender and pour it out. Since all meetings begin with the Serenity Prayer, I think I'd call it Serenity Church, so that 'my people' would know it's for us."

The great hurdle for me in those early days was Step One: "We admitted that we're powerless over our addiction and that our lives have become unmanageable." That was horrifying to me. The faith tradition that I come from had taught me my entire life that that "the age of miracles is over". The last miraculous healing took place with the last Apostle. When the Apostles died—supernatural intervention by God ceased. We all knew that "God could" but had no theology that "God would". The Holy Spirit was not a miraculous, supernatural, gift giving, miracle-working presence in our lives. As I said earlier, he was essentially a retired author. He wrote a wonderful book of instructions and dropped it in our laps. He told us to read it carefully, follow it closely, and He'd meet us on the other side to review how we did.

So...to admit that I was "powerless" over this thing that was destroying me meant that all was lost. If I couldn't find a way to dig me out of this hole, and yank myself up by my bootstraps, then there was no hope for me.

Not long ago, I ran into a buddy of mine from that group in those early days. He just smiled and asked me: "So, John, do you still hate powerless?!" We both had a good chuckle over that. In those early days, every time I shared in a meeting I'd introduce myself with the same words: "Hi, I'm John, I'm an addict and I hate powerless!"

Those first few months were hopeful and hopeless, peaceful and frustrating, joyful and frightening. Finally, all the hope of those meetings, and the love of those people, was not enough. None of that took away the constant recurring need to be numb and make it all go away.

One night, in late April, I was chairing a group meeting in a side room. At the tail end of the meeting it came my turn to share and I just snapped. I said: "I'm done with this. I'm a drug addict. That's how I cope. I'm sick and tired of telling my body it can't have what it's screaming for. The minute this meeting is over I'm going to find my dope dealer. I'm going to get me some. I'm done."

We still had to go back in the big room and join the other circles to dismiss. I knew that when we did those folks were going to try everything in their power to stop me. I didn't want to be stopped. I put myself in the back of the crowd going through the door, slipped out the back door, crawled over a septic tank, jumped a fence, and made it to my car without being stopped.

I drove down to the corner to the nearest 7-11 with a pay phone and called my dealer. After he expressed his delight and surprise to hear from me, he spoke the worst words an addict can hear: "I'm sorry, John, I just sold my last bag. I should have some more in a couple of days. You want to check back with me then?"... A couple of days?! There's no such thing as a "couple of days later" for an addict who's desperate to get high. I just hung up the phone and sat down on the sidewalk in the middle of cigarette butts and spilled Slurpee goo...and cried like a baby.

A few days later, I got a frantic call at my office from a man in our church. His son had been a leader in our youth group. A really remarkable kid. He had gone off that year to one of our denomination's universities. He had been caught smoking pot in the dorm and they had expelled him. He showed up at home last night high. They had no idea what to do. Did I have any advice for them? He could not have imagined the irony of that phone call to me. He was just frantic and turning to his pastor for help.

I had a close friend in my "home group" who had recently gone to work for a little treatment center in a tiny town a couple of hours out in the country. He had told me how excited he was about this program. A little community hospital had closed and they had made arrangements to rent it. It had been staffed with nothing but people in recovery. The counselors, cooks, nurses, right down to the janitors, were all people in recovery.

It was the only solution I could come up with on the spur of the moment. I told him that I had a buddy who was working with a program that was apparently a really special place. If I could get his son there, were they willing to have him go spend some weeks there and would they cover whatever the expense was? "Absolutely", he said, "please do whatever you can to get him there. We left him asleep when we went to work this morning. The front door is unlocked."

A few minutes later, I walked through that front door and sure enough their son was passed out in his room. He reeked of pot. I felt like I'd been punched in the gut. I knew that I desperately missed it. It wasn't until that moment that I really knew how much. I woke him up and told him we were going to get in my car and go get help for him...but, first, we needed to get rid of any dope he had in the house.

He reluctantly reached under his bed and pulled out a big bag of fresh pot. I walked into the bathroom, opened the bag to dump it in the toilet, and the aroma made me weak in the knees. I yelled for him to come in the bathroom, and while he stood there watching me, I was able to flush it. We packed some clothes and toiletries and then I got in my car for the 2-hour drive with a stoned teenager reeking of pot.

When we finally got there, I waited while they checked him in and made sure his folks were contacted. All of the appropriate papers were signed, and then I began to find my way out of that building in a fog.

One of the counselors, an amazing lady with many years of recovery, walked me to the door. As I was ready to walk out, she took me by the arm, looked me right in the eye and said: "you're not alright, are you?" I don't know that I actually screamed my reply but that's definitely how I remember it. "NO...I'M... NOT!" She asked me if I'd like to talk about it. I mumbled that I definitely would.

She led me to her office and listened while I told her my story. When I finished, she leaned forward and said: "I really think you need to come stay with us for a while. It'll take a month or so for us to teach you what you need to know. Seriously, prayerfully, consider doing that."

On the drive home I was overwhelmed by how wonderful it would be to spend some time in that place with those amazing people who could help me find the pieces that I was missing. I also knew that the consequences of that decision would be enormous. That night, after we had the kids asleep, Kay and I sat down and I told her about the day.

When I finished she asked me: "Do you need to go spend some time there?" I told her that I really thought that I did. "Well, then, you need to call them and arrange it."

I said: "Honey, it's just not that simple. They're talking about several weeks. I can't just disappear for weeks. People are going to notice that their preacher is not in the pulpit. What am I going to tell them?"

She didn't flinch. "If we could put Jesus right there on the couch and ask Him that question, what do you think He'd say?

I'm pretty sure what He'd tell you to do. 'Confess to one another, and pray for one another, so that you may be healed.' It's one thing to hide doing wrong. It's something else entirely to hide desperately trying to do right."

I let that sink in and then brought it back to some harsh reality. "You do realize that if I stand up in front of those folks and share all of this with them—that may very well be the last time I'm ever allowed to stand in that pulpit? It may be the last time I ever preach again. I just don't know of any churches who list 'recovering junkie' in their job description."

She didn't miss a beat. "The bottom line is that it's the right thing to do. If we find out it was wrong—to do right—in that church I don't want to raise my children there, anyway."

Later that week I called an Elder's meeting, sat them down around the big oak table in the Elder's Conference Room, and told them my story. In our tradition, pastors/preachers had no spiritual authority in a local church. All of that rested in the hands of laypeople in each congregation who serve as a board of Elders. I was putting the outcome in their hands.

When I finished telling them everything, there was a long stunned silence and then the initial response: "There's just no reason to get up and spill your guts to the whole church. They don't need to know all of this. You can just take a few weeks leave-of-absence, go do what you need to do, and then come back and get back to work."

I told them that was not an option. It's just not how Scripture says to handle this. After a long time of heated discussion and angry outbursts, they came to the conclusion that they'd support my decision. If I was going to stand up in front of the church and share all of this, they'd come stand beside me as a unified show of support. I was thrilled and flabbergasted. That was more than I could have possibly hoped for.

The next couple of days were a blur of preparation. I called my folks, who were working with a church in Upstate New York, and told them the whole story. Their response was an unqualified out-pouring of love and grace. I told my NA group what I was about to do and asked for their prayers. I made arrangements with my buddy who worked for the treatment center to pick me up at our house Sunday afternoon and drive me to the center. Gail Fenter, Kay's dearest friend, drove up from San Antonio to be beside her through what we were about to face.

That Sunday morning, May the 8th, as I drove to the church I knew that my life was never going to be the same. I didn't know what that meant—but I knew it was going to be very different from now on.

A few minutes before the service started, two of the Elders pulled me aside and told me that they'd all had a change of heart. If I was going to do this, none of them wanted to be seen standing there with me. I was on my own.

I walked into that cavernous sanctuary and looked around. Packed house. Mother's Day. The first thing I noticed was that the front row was packed with friends from my NA group. They looked astoundingly out of place in that room. Most of them hadn't been in a church building in years. They had all come to encourage me in the scariest moment of my life. I looked over and saw Kay with absolute resolve in her eyes...and Gail sitting beside her.

The opening parts of the service were a blur. I just leaned against a back wall and shook. Finally, the "sermon time" came and I walked that long aisle, stepped up into the pulpit, and began with a reading from Romans:

"I do not understand what I do. For what I want to do I do not do, but what I hate I do. And if I do what I do not want to do, I agree that the law is good. As it is, it is no longer I myself who do it, but it is sin living in me. I know that nothing good lives in me, that is, in my sinful nature. For I have the desire to do what is good, but I cannot carry it out. For what I do is not the good I want to do; no, the evil I do not want to do—this I keep on doing. Now if I do what I do not want to do, it is no longer I who do it, but it is sin living in me that does it. So I find this law at work: When I want to do good, evil is right there with me. For in my inner being I delight in God's law; but I see another law at work in the members of my body, waging war against the law of my mind and making me a prisoner of the law of sin at work within my members. What a wretched man I am! Who will rescue me from this body of death? Thanks be to God—through Jesus Christ our Lord!" Romans 7:15-25 (NIV)

Then I told the church my story. You could have heard a pin drop. Nobody moved.

When I finished, I said: "I have no idea how you're going to handle this information. I don't know what this means in my relationship with you. I don't know if I have a place here with you after this. Those are your decisions to make. There's nothing I can do about any of that. All I know is that I made a promise to God, myself, and my family nearly 6 months ago that I'm going to win this thing. I'm going to do whatever I have to do to win this. I've found something else that I think will help. I need to go get what those people can give me to fight this battle more effectively. I'm leaving this afternoon. I'll be gone for several weeks. I'd be grateful for your prayers for me and for my family."

As I stepped away from the pulpit my NA family spread across the front row rose to their feet and began to applaud. It rippled around the room and within a few seconds most of the people in the room were on their feet applauding for what seemed like forever. The service was hastily concluded and people began to pour down the aisle to meet me at the front. I stood in that spot for over an hour while people stood in line to take their turn to hug me, tell me they loved me, and that they'd be praying for me. An hour later, my buddy was at my house loading my luggage to take me on the long drive for the help I was desperately looking for.

THIRTEEN

If it wasn't real to me already, checking in to an acute-care, in-patient, chemical dependency treatment center makes it "real" in a hurry. As I brought in my suitcases, they were immediately taken away from me and every item was meticulously searched. I was told that there was a set schedule of everything in my day that must be followed to the letter. I was not allowed outside the building further than the steps at the doors without a staff escort. I was taken to my assigned room. My roommate was the teenage boy from our church that I had driven there just a few days earlier. We would became close friends in the days ahead... but the irony of a teenage pot-head rooming with his pastor in a drug treatment center was not lost on me.

The next day I was introduced to the treatment team. Since I was several months clean and sober, I didn't have to go through the usual de-tox. They plugged me in immediately to the full program of counseling, group sessions, and classes. After dinner every night we would end the day with a meeting. NA one night. AA the next. We had an hour of free time following the meeting. Back in our rooms by no later than 10:00. Lights out at 10:30.

After my first of those meetings on Monday night, I walked out and sat on the back steps–since that's as far as I was allowed to go without supervision. That moment is a freeze-frame for me that I can close my eyes and relive today. I can feel that concrete step I was sitting on and smell that late spring air. Beside me to my left was a yellow rose bush. There were two blooms on it. One on the side was open and starting to droop. On the very top was a bud just starting to open.

As I sat there, the enormity of what I made done made it hard for me to breathe. What had become of my life hit me deeper than I could have imagined. I just sat there and heaved sobs.

Would anything ever be alright for me again? Would there ever be real peace in my life again? How could I possibly make this up to my family? How could Kay ever forgive the devastation and humiliation I had brought down on us? Whatever she thought she was signing up for in a life with me certainly didn't look like this. I knew she loved me fiercely–but how much can she take? Would I ever preach again? Would anybody ever really want to hear me speak for God now? Ever again? Could God possibly use me now?

I've always struggled with the concept of "God told me". First of all, that was contrary to everything I knew and understood from the doctrine I was taught and what I preached. We believed that the last "speaking" God had done was through the last author of Scripture. When that man put his pen down, God became silent. It was all in the Book. There was no more direct communication between Heaven and Earth.

I had heard too many people credit God with saying some of the stupidest things to them. Some of the greatest wrongs in history have come as a result of "God told me..."

With all of that said, I'm a deep believer today in a God who will speak His mind and heart to His children as directly as necessary. That wall began to crumble for me that night on those steps.

As I sat there asking God those desperate questions, names of great men in Scripture began to flash through my thoughts like a slide show...Abraham, Jacob, Moses, David. What was the thread they had in common? What was their combined story? Matthew, Mark, Peter, Paul... As name after name, and story after story, flashed through me on that porch that night I saw the thread.

Every one of them was used by God in mighty, magnificent ways. But God didn't finally fulfill his purpose for any of them until after they had weathered enormous personal, moral, spiritual failures and collapses. When each of them gave God the shrapnel of their lives–God rebuilt them from the pieces into what He wanted them to be.

I knew that night, for sure, that God wanted that to be my story, too. It wasn't "over" for me. Maybe God's purpose for me hadn't even started yet. What I needed to learn now was how to turn my broken pieces over to Him and give Him room to rebuild them into what He had in mind all along. Whatever that was. But how do I do that?

The master treatment plan in the program there was to lead each of us through the first three of the Twelve Steps...and then send us home prepared to start work on the 4th Step. When the treatment team unanimously agreed that we had thoroughly "worked" those three steps and had made them part of our lives and recovery, we "graduated" from the in-patient part of the program. We'd go home then, and the staff in their "after care" offices back in the city would work with us on the next chapter of our journey. We could expect to be in the in-patient program roughly 28 days. That could significantly vary, though. The bottom line was not how many days we were there. It was how thoroughly we had woven those 3 principles into our lives.

That immediately ran me head-long into a brick wall. Step One was the hurdle I simply couldn't get over: "We admitted that we were powerless over our addiction—that our lives had become unmanageable." If I'm "powerless" over all of this, then there's no hope for me. God can't be expected to step down personally into the middle of this mess I've made of my life. We're talking "supernatural intervention" here. He doesn't do that kind of thing anymore.

The staff worked relentlessly with me to help me jump that hurdle. I worked frantically to get where they were trying to take me. I just simply had no concept of how that could work. I had no place to put it.

Those weeks were saturated with some pretty outrageous out-pouring of grace. I was so worried about my family back home. Kay was a school teacher, in the final weeks of her school year, with two children to take care of. My mom and dad were living in Upstate New York—serving a mission church there. My dad dropped everything and flew to Texas to help Kay pick up the pieces and take care of the kids.

The mail. I doubt that small town post office had ever seen anything like it. Hundreds of cards and letters poured in from all over the country. Word had spread fast and people flooded me with words of love, support, and encouragement. One day, the director of the program brought an armload of mail to my room and was laughing as he walked through the door. He said: "the postmaster at the local post office stopped me when I came in this morning and wanted to know what kind of celebrity it is we're housing over here!"

One afternoon between sessions, the director came to my room and said: "There's somebody here to see you. We usually don't allow visitors except for the designated times on week-ends—but he says he's come a long way." I walked into the front reception parlor and directly into a bear-hug from my friend Pat.

Pat and I met, and become lifelong friends, while we were both in our 20s pastoring churches in the same neighborhood in Joliet, Illinois. We haven't lived on the same side of the Missis-sippi River since 1980 but have remained closer than brothers ever since.

One day, shortly after I checked myself into the treatment center, he called my office just to check in and chat. My secre-tary knew how close we were and told him what had happened and where I was. At the time, he was pastoring a church in the Illinois suburbs of St. Louis. He went home, packed a bag, and caught the first flight to Dallas. When he landed, he rented a car and drove to our house to check on Kay and the kids. Then he drove the 2 hours out into the country to walk through that door and ask to see me. We spent an hour together. He told me how much he loved me and that nothing could ever change that. He told me that he believed in me and that God was going to bring great good out of all of this. We prayed together. He got back in his rental car, drove hours back to the airport, and flew home.

There were extraordinary moments of light and grace in that dark time.

My 22nd day there the staff was still not convinced that I had accepted or come to grips with my "powerlessness". Going home in the standard 28 days was starting to look pretty hopeless. By the grace of God, that was also the first day on the job for a new counselor on the treatment team.

They sat her down to give her the rundown on the current patients. As she told me the story later, it went something like this: "And then we have this preacher from the Dallas area. He's trying really hard. He's not fighting us. He's doing everything we ask him to do. We've tried every way we know how but he cannot let go and accept his powerlessness. We're stuck on Step One and we just can't get him there." She asked what kind of church I pastored. They told her. She just smiled and said: "Let me have a crack at him."

That afternoon, Sandra (her actual name–she could care less about her anonymity and I want her to have full credit here!) took me out and sat me down at a picnic table behind the clinic. She leaned forward, looked me square in the eye, and said: "I know the faith tradition you come from. I was raised in that same tradition. I know what you were taught. I know what you believe–and why you believe it. Those are really good people. They love God deeply and they love you. Because of how much they love you both they introduced you to Him the best they could. Now, listen to me very carefully. They taught you the truth as they understood it. They meant well...but they were wrong. It's not true. God has not retired from the miracle business. He'll still step in supernaturally to do for us what we can't do for ourselves. He'll change the course of nature for us. Until you understand that...and let Him...you're never going to be alright."

At that moment it all clicked, the pieces finally fell into place, and I got it. The next day the staff "passed me" on Step One.

Step Two automatically fell into place on top of it. "We came to believe that a Power greater than ourselves could restore us to sanity." My belief in God had never been a problem for me. I have always believed in Him. I never questioned His power. I always knew that God could...I just had no confidence that He would.

Two days after my visit with Sandra at the picnic table my counselor walked me across the street to a beautiful old church. He had been given the key to the sanctuary by the pastor there for moments like this. We walked together to the front of the sanctuary and knelt together at the altar that was flooded with light from 100 year-old stained glass on all sides of us. He reached in his pocket and pulled out a copy of the Third Step Prayer from page 63 of the "Big Book" of Alcoholics Anonymous and we prayed it out loud together...

"God, I offer myself to Thee-to build with me and to do with me as Thou wilt. Relieve me of the bondage of self, that I may better do Thy will. Take away my difficulties, that victory over them may bear witness to those I would help of Thy Power, Thy Love, and Thy Way of life. May I do Thy will always!"

Although there were some dizzying spiritual highs still to come, that was the most profound face-to-face encounter with God I had ever experienced up to that moment.

Confident that I finally "got it", the staff voted unanimously to "graduate" me. I went home three days early.

FOURTEEN

As soon as I got home Kay, the kids, and I flew to New York to spend some time with my folks. It was a perfect time. My mom and dad would load us up every day to go have adventures. They had located a local group for me to attend every night. It was the closest thing to "normal" that I had felt in a long time.

If my last experiences at the treatment center were a dizzy spiritual high...the first days back with our church were a crash landing. The day we got back from New York I was called to a meeting with the Elders. We gathered around that big oak table and they outlined for me a list of decisions they had made. They said: "We don't know what to do about you—but until we decide, this is how it's going to be:

...You are not allowed to preach or teach—here or anywhere else.

...You are not allowed to publish anything you write in our church bulletin or anywhere else.

...You are not allowed to perform weddings, conduct funerals, baptize anybody or pray out loud in public.

...We have arranged for you to meet weekly with a counselor we have chosen. His practice is in (a city 3 hours away). You will drive to where he is and meet with him every Tuesday. You will sign all of the appropriate waivers so that he can discuss with us any questions we may have about you and your recovery.

...Effective immediately, we are reducing your salary by 1/3. Since you are not permitted to perform your usual ministry functions, we will make a list of chores for you to do. There are any number of things that need doing that people don't want to volunteer for–such as stacking boxes and cleaning out the benevolence warehouse. That sort of humbling will probably do you good.

...You will not attend our regular meetings as you have in the past. We have assigned 2 of us to meet with you regularly and report back to the rest of us whatever we need to know.

...If we get word of you complaining about any of this, we will stop your reduced salary immediately and ask you to clear out your office. Are there any questions?"

I couldn't think of any. I stumbled home numb that night and told Kay what the decisions were. She was furious. I was shell-shocked.

The first practical thing we had to address was how to live on a radically reduced income. Like most young couples we pretty much lived paycheck-to-paycheck. In fact, we had been living significantly "beyond our means". I wanted to see this through and find out if redemption there could really happen. How was that going to even be possible?

Word spread quickly through the congregation what was happening. A couple of nights later two of our Deacons showed up at our front door together. They said: "We've been hearing some very disturbing rumors about some decisions that have been made about you." They rattled off several things they had heard and asked me if that was accurate. I told them it was. They asked me how much my salary had been cut. I told them.

They said: "You probably want to do nothing but flee right about now. That's certainly how we'd feel. We're here to beg you not to. Please don't. This is a large, influential church. People all over the country are watching us to see how we handle this. We can't let this be our answer. If our response to you asking for our help is to do as much damage to you as possible...what idiot would ever come to us asking for spiritual help again? Please give us some time to help them see how wrong this is. We'll see to it that your family doesn't suffer in the meantime. The two of us will show up at your door every Monday with two checks to cover what they're taking from your salary. Please give us time to try to turn this in the right direction."

I told them I agreed and I would. They both wrote checks, handed them to me, hugged Kay and me, and left. Every Monday for the months that followed they showed up at our door with two checks.

For the next several months we tried to do the next right thing. I showed up at the office every morning and did the chores they had lined up for me. Every Sunday I sat in the pew with my family. Every Tuesday I spent 6 hours in the car for an hour with the counselor they had selected. He turned out to be a Godsend. He was an incredibly encouraging man who was baffled by all of this. Late in the summer they flew him in for a report on my progress. He told them I was doing all the things it takes for long term recovery. He truly believed I was going to be alright. They told me to keep going. With the Elder's permission I started a weekly Bible Study for a growing crowd from my NA group. I went to meetings every night.

FIFTEEN

Where I was really stalled was in my Step work. The staff at the treatment center had been a little overly enthusiastic in preparing me to go home and do my 4th Step: "We made a searching and fearless moral inventory of ourselves". One of the counselors had given me a 4th Step Workbook, another had given me a set of tapes, another some charts and a book to read. I was thoroughly confused.

One day, with all of that spread across my desk, I called my sponsor and asked if he could stop by after work and help me make sense out of all of this. He walked in my office and I showed him all of the materials I'd been given to help me. Without a word he walked over to my desk, put his arm on one side of my desk, dragged his arm across, and dumped everything in a pile on the floor. You have to understand here that I'm a diagnosed obsessive/compulsive. Primary symptom? Compulsive tidiness. This was a tough moment for me!

He asked me for my "Big Book". I reached over on the shelf and handed him my copy of "Alcoholics Anonymous". "This is not rocket science", he said, "and nobody should make it complicated. Remember this was all designed to be simple enough for brain-fried folks like us to completely understand and practice. It'll be some of the toughest work you've ever done. It's hard...but it's simple enough for a child to understand."

He turned to page 64 and had me read the next couple of pages. The heart of it is the sentence: "Resentment is the number one offender!" A lot of research has been done over the years that has shown that the emotion most likely to trigger an addict is "resentment". Research wasn't necessary for that first handful gathered around Dr. Bob's table. As they shared their stories, there was always a common thread. When one of us is in the most danger is when there are unresolved resentments toward somebody or some thing in our lives.

My sponsor had me buy a 4-subject spiral notebook. In the first section, he had me draw lines from top to bottom creating three columns on the page. At the top of column one he had me write the words: "I resent..." One the top of column two we wrote: "Caused by..." At the top of column three: "Affects my..."

We turned to the second section of the notebook. He asked me when my earliest memories are. I said around age 4. He said at the top of the first page in this section write: "Age 4". On the top of the next page write: "Age 5". Continue on with a page for every year of my life until now.

We turned to the third section. At the top he had me write: "My Wrongs..." He explained that it was the only heading this section needed. He said that the purpose of the 4th section of the notebook would come up at a later time.

With that done, he said: "I want you to dedicate 20 minutes a day to this. No more than that because it's easy to start 'wallowing' in this and there's no healing in wallowing. Sit down in a quiet place and pick one of those years of your life in Section Two. Remember that time and place in your life. Where were you? Who did you spend time with? What were you doing?

"Now, be completely honest. Did some person or thing hurt you during that time in your life? Did you do wrong that may have hurt you or somebody else. Write those things down on that page. Pick another year of your life and do the same thing... and another...but never more than 20 minutes of this in a day. You'll drown in it.

"When you have thoroughly and completely relived those times and places—when you have listed in detail the hurts that you caused and those that hurt you—then transfer them to section one or section three.

"If it was a hurt you received, write that name in column one. Beside it, in column two, write down the specific details of what happened to hurt you. What specifically "caused" this hurt and resentment? Beside each of those, in column three, write down how you were "affected" by that happening to you. There's a great list of the ways these wounds affect us on the bottom of page 64 and the top of page 65 in the "Big Book".

"Now comes the really painful honesty. As we relive each of those chapters of our lives, we're going to dig up our own "wrongs". What have we done to hurt God, ourselves, or others? In as much detail as possible we need to list those times, places and people in the third section of our notebook. Time by time, occasion by occasion, incident by incident."

My sponsor was dead-on right when he said this process is "simple enough for a child to understand and the hardest thing you'll ever do." It took most of the rest of that summer. 20 minutes at a time. Reliving my life: place by place, person by person, year by year. All of the hurt inflicted on me and all the damage I had done.

SIXTEEN

When I was convinced that I had done as "searching and fearless" a moral inventory as I was capable of producing—it was time to move on to Step Five: "We admitted to God, to ourselves, and to another human being the exact nature of our wrongs." I was going to have to tell all of this to somebody. I found that possibility to be absolutely horrifying!

I knew how profoundly Biblical this concept was. Kay had quoted those very words from Scripture the night we made the decision to share our struggle with our church. James 5:16, "Therefore, confess your sins to each other and pray for each other so that you may be healed". That's good in theory—but now I was expected to speak all of the garbage of my life to SOMEBODY!!

My sponsor and I agreed that the requirements for somebody to share all of this with was: 1) Somebody I could trust absolutely... 2) Someone who understood this journey through the Steps and what I was trying to accomplish here... 3) Somebody who could help me connect this experience with the Steps that follow it.

I added one more. I very much wanted it to be somebody that I didn't have to look at the next day...or pretty much any day! After a lot of prayerful consideration I settled on my counselor back at the treatment center. He and I had become really close through my weeks in his care. He had many years of recovery himself. He was literally a professional in leading people through this journey. I not only trusted him—but, by law, he could never repeat what I shared with him. The primary selling point for me? He lived over 100 miles away and I wouldn't have to see him regularly when it was over!

I do look back on all of that fear, trepidation, and personal drama and chuckle at myself today. In the decades since then I've been on the receiving/listening end of more people's 5th Steps than I can count. Many scores of them. I have never walked away from that experience with somebody and felt anything but honored to have been trusted and allowed to go into those deep places in their hearts with them. We all think we are terminally and uniquely bad. I've come to the conclusion that we flatter ourselves. None of us are that special in our badness!

I called him and told him what I needed from him. He said he'd be honored and scheduled an entire afternoon for me the next week. The day came and I drove through the country to that little clinic and had the completely unexpected feeling of coming back home to some place very special to me. He and I walked several blocks to the edge of town and stopped at a little wooden bridge over a creek. We sat on the edge of the bridge and dangled our feet over the creek; I opened my notebook and began to read.

It took me most of 3 hours to pour out all the hurt of a lifetime. How people had hurt me and how I had hurt them. The times I had failed myself and the times I had hurt God. Year by year. Incident by incident. I pulled out all of it and and spoke most of it for the first time in my life. Periodically he would pause and ask me to explain something. Other times he would say: "Now, flip over to the back of your notebook and make a

note of that. You'll need that for your 8th Step". Now I understood what my sponsor meant when he told me I'd understand
the purpose for the 4th section of my notebook later. Mostly, he
just sat there and loved me and listened.

SEVENTEEN

He told me as I finally closed my notebook that Steps 6 and 7 were not long, drawn out pieces of work like my 4th Step had been. In fact, he said, you will complete them before you go home tonight.

Step 6: "We were entirely ready to have God remove all these defects of character."

Step 7: "We humbly asked Him to remove our shortcomings."

He told me exactly what to do. On my way out of town I stopped at a convenience store and picked up a disposable lighter. Just a few minutes up the road on my way home there was a little roadside park and picnic area with a stone and concrete grill. I pulled in by the grill, carefully tore out the 4th section of the notebook, and left it in the car. I took the rest of the book with me, walked over to the grill, and sat down on the edge of it.

Ripping out the first page, I lay it down on the grill and slowly read it one last time. I allowed myself to feel all of that hurt on that page one last time. Then I prayed out loud: "God, grant me the serenity to accept those things I cannot change. Give me courage to change those things that I can. Please give me the wisdom to know the difference." Then I took out that lighter, set fire to the corner of the page, and watched it literally go up in flame and turn to ash.

Then I tore out the next page and did exactly the same thing. And the next one. And the next...

By the time I finished reliving, praying over, letting go and burning that last page I was on the most exhilarating spiritual high of my life. I burned all the blank pages, the cover of the notebook, and a hamburger wrapper that was lying on the ground! It was the first time in my life that I had truly experienced the complete and absolute release of all the hurts and garbage of my life. His "grace and mercy" were real to me for the first time. He really DOES give me what I don't deserve. He really does NOT give me what I do deserve. I felt truly "clean" for the first time in my life.

I took the last section of my notebook home with me to begin the next leg of this journey. Steps 8 and 9 are another pair that are actually two parts of the next piece of our healing.

Step 8: "We made a list of all persons we had harmed, and became willing to make amends to them all."

Step 9: "We made direct amends to such people wherever possible, except when to do so would injure them or others."

The way I had been led through Steps 4 and 5 meant that my 8th Step list was already written. As I spoke all the harm I had done, and the people I had hurt, in my 5th Step—my counselor had me flip over to that back section and list those people and things. I now had a thorough list of the people that I had harmed in my life.

Now it was time to begin the process of making right whatever I could. In some cases, it's just a sincere apology and honestly seeking their forgiveness. In others, actual restitution might be in order. Some of those people I might never be able to locate...

or they might be dead. In those cases I make a "living amends". I live my life in a way that never inflicts those kinds of wounds again.

The one critical exception to the "direct amends" is that I never have the right to hurt you to make myself feel better. If that contact with me will hurt you, then I need to resolve that with myself and God.

This is the place in the journey where the "miracle happens". So many of us never do the hard work to get to this place and stop short of the miracle. How incredibly tragic it is for us to miss it.

One of the most loved principles in recovery fellowships of all kinds is a quote from the AA "Big Book" in the middle of the section describing the making of our 9th Step amends. It's come to be known as the "12 Promises". It describes what we can expect to happen during this cleaning up of the wreckage of our lives. We close every service of Serenity Church with a reverent reading of these words. We open every meeting of our Overcomers Fellowship with these same words. It says:

"If we are painstaking about this phase of our development, we will be amazed before we are half way through. We are going to know a new freedom and a new happiness. We will not regret the past nor wish to shut the door on it. We will comprehend the word serenity and we will know peace. No matter how far down the scale we have gone, we will see how our experience can benefit others. That feeling of uselessness and self-pity will disappear. We will lose interest in selfish things and gain interest in our fellows. Self-seeking will slip away. Our whole attitude and outlook upon life will change. Fear of people and of economic insecurity will leave us. We will intuitively know how to handle situations which used to baffle us. We will suddenly realize that God is doing for us what we could not do for ourselves.

Are these extravagant promises? We think not. They are being fulfilled among us-sometimes quickly, sometimes slowly. They will always materialize if we work for them."

The first time I heard those words spoken was in a meeting during my time at the treatment center. I thought that was absolute nonsense. There's simply no way that all of that could happen for me. I couldn't even imagine a life that looked like that. I tell the world today how very wrong I was. Every bit of that is the reality of my life today. That miracle that we're promised is very real.

EIGHTEEN

Not long after that miracle on the side of the road, one of the two Elders who had been assigned to communicate with me came to our house. My punishment, and removal from preaching, had been going on for nearly 5 months now.

He seemed incredibly upbeat. He sat down with Kay and me in our living room and told us that it looked like we were coming to an end to this chapter. They were so proud of how I had handled myself during this time. They had been regularly in touch with the counselor I had been traveling to see every week. They had long visits with the staff of the treatment center. Everyone involved in my recovery was very encouraging and convinced that I was doing everything necessary to live my life in long-term recovery. He leaned back with a big smile and said: "I think you can expect to be returned to our pulpit and your ministry with us very soon."

Kay and I were overwhelmed that this nightmare could really be winding up and life could return to some kind of "normal" again. We were so excited we could hardly sleep that night.

Two days later, I was called to a meeting with all of the Elders. It was my first time to meet with the group of them since that incredibly painful meeting the week I came back from treatment.

They had selected a spokesman who got right to business. He said: "John, we want you to know that we're very proud of you. We appreciate the hard work you've done to fight and win this battle you're in. You've shown a lot of humility in following everything we've asked you to do since you've been back. We've been in touch with the people who are working with you in your recovery. They're very positive that your chances for long term success are excellent..."

Then the other shoe dropped. "However...after much discussion, we have come to a unanimous agreement that you can never be effective here again. We want to begin the process of transitioning you to a ministry somewhere else. We feel that the best way to handle that is for you to resign. Feeling as positively as we do about you and your recovery—we're prepared to give you an unqualified recommendation to another church. We will continue your reduced salary for a reasonable amount of time while you search for another ministry."

I was speechless. When I caught my breath, I turned to the man who had come to our house to tell me that I was about to be restored to that pulpit. I asked him: "He said this is a unanimous decision. That includes you?"... "It does"... "Didn't you come to my house two days ago and tell me..." ... "I gave it more thought and changed my mind."

The spokesman stepped back in. "We're prepared to give you a wonderful recommendation." I gave that a moment to sink in and said: "Let me make sure I understand this. What would be the crux of that recommendation? We don't want this junkie in our pulpit, but we'd love to see him in yours?"

"John, we believe that it would be best for the church for you to stand up in front of them and tell them that this is your decision, and you have decided to resign. That could greatly affect how much we support you in your transition."

I said: "Brothers, that just wouldn't be honest. They've watched how hard I've worked to be restored to my place in this Family. If you feel this is right, you need to tell them so."

There wasn't much more to be said. I drove home slowly and tried to make sense out of what had just happened. When I walked in the door Kay looked at me excitedly and said: "So, what did they say?!"... "They fired me"... She laughed. "No, really, what did they say?!" ... "Really. They fired me"... It was a long, sad, confused, angry night at our house.

The next day, I picked up the phone and called my buddy who managed the city offices of the treatment center and was now one of the owners of the program. They had been offering me a job since almost as soon as I came home from the clinic. The most recent discussions had been "just name your price—we really need you on this team." I told him what had happened. His immediate response: "So, are you ready to come work with us? Name a salary and can you start Monday?"

I told him what I was making before my my salary was cut. He told me they'd match that and add some to it. My job would be working with recovering people and their families out of their main offices less than 10 minutes from what had been my church office. He would train me to lead interventions. I would teach after-care classes helping recent graduates from the in-patient program continue their recovery. I'd work with their families—educating them in the nature of our sickness and preparing them for their loved one's new life in recovery.

It sounded perfect to me. I had such deep love and respect for the whole team I'd be working with. They had changed my life. Now I'd have the chance to work with them to do the same thing for other people like me. I told him I'd need a few weeks to regroup and spend some time with my family. I'd start work in a month. Those were sweet weeks. There was the uncertainty of a whole new thing in our future–but at least we were no longer in limbo. We knew what the future looked like. We knew what cards we had to play.

Just as I was ready to start my new job, I got a call from a man I had never met. He introduced himself as an Elder at a church in a little county-seat town about an hour away. They were searching for a new preacher/minister for their church. Would I be willing to talk to them?

I asked him the obvious question: "How much do you know about my life lately?" He replied that they knew it all. His daughter and son-in-law were active members of the church we were leaving. He had followed my story very closely. He said: "Honestly, that's why we're calling you. We believe you probably have some new things to offer people that we really need."

This seemed way too good to be true...but I knew I had to at least investigate what was happening here. We set up a time to meet, get to know each other, and talk about it. We met and spent hours together discussing my life and how fundamentally I had changed. They described a church in transition. They had been an old-line, old-school, church of our denomination, but they had a large piece of their church hungry for a new message of hope. We made arrangements for our family to come be with them for a Sunday, have me preach for them, and get to know each other. At the end of that day we sat down again, and they offered me the ministry at their church.

NINETEEN

Now I had no idea what direction God was pointing me. I was starting a new job that week, using everything God had taught me through all of this to help save the lives of other people like me. On the other hand, I knew that God had made me to preach. Through all of these months there had been a gaping hole in me where "preaching" belonged. Add to all of that the fact that Kay and I were still bleeding from recent wounds from church folks.

After a lot of prayer and struggle we decided to try a compromise. I went back to those Elders and said: "Kay and I just aren't ready to give our hearts to another church yet. We're still healing from some deep wounds. I just started a new job with some people I love deeply–doing something I believe in passionately. I'd like to suggest that we date each other for a while before we get married. We need to know that we can trust you. We need to know that we're safe here. The church owns a parsonage. Put some beds and a table in there for us. We'll come spend our weekends here and I'll preach for you. Let me serve the church part-time for a while. I'll continue my work with the treatment center. If it all feels right in a few months, we'll discuss it again." They immediately agreed to do that.

As we moved through that Spring, we felt really comfortable. It was obvious that there were two distinct groups in that church. They literally sat on either side of the main aisle in the sanctuary. One group (we'll call them "Group One") was obviously desperate to hear a message of grace, a loving God, healing and acceptance of each other. "Group Two" mostly sat with their arms crossed and responded very little. They seemed like mostly good-hearted country folks. Maybe in time, as I unfolded how Scriptural this Gracious God really is, they'd come on this journey with us.

My work with the treatment center was sweet, incredibly rewarding, relentless and exhausting. My family saw very little of me. As the school year wound to a close, Kay and I made the decision that we were ready to make this move and return to full-time ministry. Kay was hired as a teacher at the local high school. Our pieces fell into place.

Within months of our moving, the mood began to change dramatically. About a year later, a large group of men in the church asked to meet with the Elders. I wasn't at that meeting, but the Elder who was chairing that meeting, and who remains one of my favorite people until this day, recounted it to me like this: Their appointed spokesman came right to the point and demanded that I be fired. They wanted me gone. Now.

When the Elder asked him what I had done to so offend them, he instantly replied: "If we never hear another word of that 'grace' and 'love' crap, it'll be too soon." Stunned, the Elder said: "Well, those are two deeply Biblical principles. If you don't want John to preach those things, what do you want him to preach?" The answer: "Hell. We want to hear Hell. If we come to church and leave feeling good—then we obviously haven't heard the Gospel preached."

It became crystal clear that we not only had two groups on two different pages...we were in completely different books. That conflict got much, much, uglier in the weeks ahead. I've seen some meanness in the church in my lifetime. I've heard some horrific stories. Nothing I've seen or heard could match the ugliness that unfolded in that place. I began to write that story here and decided that I simply don't want to relive it long enough to type it. To wallow in that doesn't add anything helpful to this story of hope.

A large group finally came to the Elders and said: "We're done. We've watched so many people wounded through the years. We've watched generations of children grow up in that ugliness and flee the first chance they got. They can't have our kids, too. We're asking our Elders to shepherd us out of that and into freedom. Will you do it?" They committed to lead them out.

The Elders then came to me and my friend Monty, our youth minister, and asked for our help. They needed us. Would we do this new thing with them? Monty and Tamaria...and Kay and I...believed there was no other solution. Maybe we were brought here for this very purpose.

By this time, I was the officer in the local Lions Club in charge of renting out the Lions Club Hall just off the courthouse square. It was a big, open, meeting room with lots of folding chairs. Since I kept the calendar, I knew it was not rented out on Sunday. We scheduled our first service there the following Sunday morning. We sent out word that anyone looking for the message of grace, love, hope and freedom would find it there.

It was a sunny, bitterly cold, morning in early January when several of us got there to set things up. We really had no idea who, or how many, would walk through that door. We were thrilled and flabbergasted when 128 people poured through that door into a room that would comfortably hold 100. Several had to stand against the wall through the entire service. There was simply no place to seat them.

The defining moment for me that day was when the oldest couple in our church walked through the door. They were both nearly 90 and had been in that church since they were children. She was leaning on a cane. He was slowly shuffling behind a walker. She slowly walked over to me, gave me a big hug, then looked me square in the eye and said: "John, are we finally free?" I replied: "Yes, ma'am, I think we are." She said: "Then I can die in peace." She turned around and found her seat.

TWENTY

We stayed for 6 more years to help that church grow and sink roots. It was the happiest time of my life up to that point. It was there that God began to teach me how recovery and the church belong together.

We began a new 12-Step group that we called the "Overcomers Fellowship". It worked just like any other 12-step recovery group with two major exceptions.

We freely identify our Higher Power as Jesus Christ. We call Him by name. We believe that He's in attendance in our meetings. We talk to Him directly in our meetings—often.

The 2nd difference is that anybody with something destructive in their lives that they can't just "will away" qualifies to belong in our fellowship. I've said countless times that to my knowledge that includes everybody I've met in my life so far! Doesn't it? I don't know anybody whose life wouldn't be sweeter, and their relationship with God wouldn't be closer, as a result of following that way of life.

We were told early on that it wouldn't work to mix people with different struggles in the same meeting. Alcoholics need to be in meetings only with other alcoholics. Drug addicts with other drug addicts. Sex addicts with other sex addicts. Co-dependents with other co-dependents...etc, etc, etc.

Over 20 years of experience now has proven to us that's just not true. We all have the same spiritual sickness: "We're powerless over things that hurt us and our lives are not manageable by us." The symptoms may vary—but the disease and the treatment are the same.

We began that group with 4 of us sitting in our living room. In the years that followed that group grew to scores of us crammed into a room the same size. There were usually as many reasons for being there as there were people in the room. People dealing with addictions to everything imaginable...sitting side-by-side with people overwhelmed by divorce, grief, depression, despair and hopelessness of every kind. All of us were the same. We were "powerless" and the same 12 solutions lift all of us out of those pits.

Our new baby church bought four, old, dilapidated buildings from the local Catholic church who had moved into beautiful new facilities on the edge of town. Some of my sweetest memories are the carloads of people who would pull up after work. They'd unload a picnic dinner, tools, paintbrushes...eat a quick bite and then move on to the next project in rebuilding and remodeling those old buildings from the ground up. We'd sing, we'd visit, we'd laugh—a lot. God used those times to mold a hurting group of spiritual refugees into a family. There's a special, deep, undefinable joy shared by people who have spent their lives in bondage and are suddenly set free. It was a giddy time.

Those old buildings turned out more beautifully than we could have hoped or imagined. One of the first ones we completed became a recovery center for the community. At that time, there was no NA group in the area. I helped to do an intervention on one of the men in our church who was now home from treatment. We chartered an NA group and committed that we would meet and have a meeting if it was just the two of us. For what seemed like a long time, that's exactly what it was... the two of us.

Finally, a nurse from the local hospital walked in one night. She'd been caught stealing narcotics at the hospital. Part of the requirements of her probation was to attend meetings. We were thrilled! We hadn't formed a circle yet—but our new group was at least a triangle. Today, that group is one of the largest and most active in that part of the state—with meetings every night of the week. My buddy who first sat there with me, fresh home from treatment, now has over 20 years of sobriety and is the very heart of that fellowship.

About this time, Sandra (yep, THAT Sandra...she of the picnic table epiphany!) and her husband moved to town. They had been hired as the counseling team for the chemical dependency recovery program at a State prison in the area. She immediately plugged into our new Overcomers Group and became one of the real rocks in our growing recovery ministry.

She came to me early on and said that there was a critical need in the program at the prison that they needed my help with. The men that they were working with were deeply committed to their recovery and were faithfully working their way through the Steps. They hit a brick wall, though, when it came time to do their 5th Step. Most of them had things in their 4th Step inventories that, if the wrong people knew them, would buy them serious additional prison time, fresh charges, new problems with the law.

As much as they admired and appreciated their counselors—they were employees of the prison and part of "the system". They were simply not ready to admit the "exact nature" of all of their wrongs to them.

What they decided they needed was someone who the inmates knew for sure would faithfully protect their confidentiality. They understood that "clergy confidentiality" is rigorously protected by the law. However, not just any clergy would know how to lead them through this process. It needed to be somebody with deep personal experience in the 12-Step journey. Put all of that together, and in that part of the world they came up with a short list of...me.

For the next several years I became the designated 5th Step recipient for all of the men in that prison. I spent countless hours in a tiny little holding cell listening to those men pour out their hurts and wrongs. I looked back more than once and chuckled at myself for how terrified I had been to speak mine out loud. Could anybody know those things about me and not hate me? Obviously, I heard things in that little cell that made me feel like an "amateur" sinner! I never once walked out of there feeling anything but profoundly honored that those men would allow me into the deepest, most wounded, places in their hearts.

I have a dear friend at Serenity Church, with many years of recovery, who has also been on the receiving end of more 5th Step confessions than she can count or remember. I've heard her say that she can't remember the details of any of them. It's like some kind of "Divine amnesia" sets in when that moment is over. That has been exactly my experience. Of the scores of 5th Steps I have heard through the years—I can't recall the details of any of them. It's my role in that sacred moment to hear... and then forget. Exactly the way God listens to us pour out the the wrongs and ugliness of our lives to Him...and then forgets. God said: "This is the covenant I will make with them... their sins and lawless acts I will remember no more." (Hebrews 10:16-17)

As one of the "least anonymous" recovering people in a small town, I became the go-to-guy for an incredible array of situations that came up through the years. One of my favorites was the time a group of the leaders in our high school got caught at a party where there was some drinking. These were good kids that included everybody from the Student Body President to the class Valedictorian. The principal knew that expelling all of them was serious over-kill, but there had to be a serious response from the school that made an undeniable statement that this was not acceptable.

She called me and asked me to drop by her office. When I got there she said: "John, these are good kids. They have remarkable futures ahead of them that we could permanently damage with the wrong response here. At the same time, we can't just let this slide. Here's what I'm thinking: I'd like to require them to attend several weeks of classes on the dangers of drugs and alcohol after school. Would you be willing to teach and lead those classes?"

I agreed to do that, and for the next several weeks had the whole crowd of them as my captive audience. They're all in their 30s now. I've kept up with most of them and they are living good lives...including the boy (the Valedictorian) who would grow up and marry my daughter! He strenuously denied then, and now, that he was actually drinking at that party. He's an honest man and I believe him...but I have to love the circumstances that put the future daddy of my grandchildren in front of me for weeks after school!

During these years, my mom and dad decided it was time to retire. They had been living for years in New York and were ready to come back home to Texas. My sister lived in Ft. Worth just 30 minutes away from us. Our two kids are their only grandchildren. They bought a house around the corner from us so we could all enjoy these years together. It was a wonderful time. If "grandparenting" was an Olympic sport, they'd both have gold medals!

They both got immediately, deeply, involved in our church. I've described how spiritually rigid my upbringing was. The sweet part of that story is that they both lived long enough to find, and excitedly embrace, spiritual freedom. After so many years of oppressive legalism, they were almost beside themselves to finally be let out of that cage and truly set free.

That "retirement" business, though, didn't work out so well! They were neither one "retired" kind of people. Shortly after they moved to town, my mom went to work as an assistant to the County Sheriff. My dad began to do volunteer chaplain ministry at the local prison. Almost immediately, he was offered the position as the full-time staff chaplain and spent the next few years loving on those broken men behind bars. When he retired the 2nd time, he joined my mom at the County Jail as the chaplain there.

After my dad died in March of 1999, the Sheriff came to my mom and said: "We've really struggled with who could possibly replace him here. He had the most amazing combination of strength, compassion, and wisdom. He never took any foolishness from our inmates—but he made sure they always understood that their lives had real value. Who could we possibly find to replace all of that? The only answer we could come up with is...

you." By the time you read this, my mom will be in her 80s. She still walks into that jail every morning dispensing hope to those broken people behind bars.

Finally, 8 years into our ministry there, we knew it was time for a fresh challenge. I had promised to stay there until that baby church was rooted and strong. It was all of those things. It is today a center of hope and healing. Too often, when a pastor leaves a ministry, it's because he's mad at those people or they're mad at him. Nothing could be further from the truth in this story. All of these years later they remain deep, true family to us. They have been faithful supporters, spiritually and financially, of Serenity Church. I just knew that it was time to take the message to a fresh audience. It was time for them to hear the message from a fresh voice.

TWENTY ONE

In the Fall of 1996, I got a call from a church that I knew well and loved in the North Dallas suburbs...less than an hour away. They were looking for a pastor. They were deeply familiar with our church. In fact, Monty who had been my ministry partner and helped us birth the church that we were serving...had been their pastor for the last 5 years. They wanted to do those same things. Monty had them well on the way. He had just accepted a call to the church he had grown up in. They wanted to keep moving as a healing community. Would I consider coming to help them do that?

We were at the right time and place in our lives to take on a new challenge. Our church was strong, established, and growing. Jenna was in her Senior year about to graduate from high school. Jay was just starting high school. The pieces all fit.

I began my preaching ministry there that winter—commuting until the end of the school year. Kay quickly found a teaching job in the high school in our new neighborhood. We moved that summer to begin an exciting new challenge.

The years that followed were really good for us. Those folks meant what they said. They really wanted to be a place of grace and healing. The first thing we did was to birth the Overcomers Fellowship there. That movement followed a pattern I had seen before. We started with a handful of us...that over the years became dozens and then scores of us.

Some of us started an NA group at our church building. A few of us, one night a week, grew into a thriving group meeting every night. An AA group was started and grew the same way. As we became recognized as a healing place, our pews began to fill up with people from those fellowships.

One of my favorite stories from those years is a young husband and daddy whose life and marriage had unraveled through years of using and selling drugs. His wife had finally reached her breaking point and said she wouldn't live around that anymore. After they separated, he just spiraled deeper down that hole until he hit absolute bottom.

They had family who were deep in recovery who lived near our church. They offered him a place to sleep on their couch for a while under the condition that he'd stay clean and sober and attend an AA meeting every day. He grew up in a family that was deeply involved in a church of our denomination in a town a couple of hours away. Every time he was driven to an AA meeting, they drove right by our church.

Even though he had been as far away from God as you can get for a long time—the importance of "church" was hard-wired into him. One Sunday morning he was in an AA meeting. When it came his turn to share, he told the group that he had reached a point in his life that he was willing to do anything to stay sober and get his life back. He was even seriously considering finding his way back to church.

Shortly before the meeting wrapped up, two of the guys in the group got up to slip out a little early. On their way out, they leaned over and whispered to him that they were on their way to church if he'd like to go with them. "No thanks", he said, "I think I've spotted the place I'm supposed to go."

When his sister-in-law picked him up from the meeting, he asked her to drop him off at that church on the way home. He walked in, sat down, and looked up to find those two guys from the meeting sitting right in front of him. He tapped them on the shoulder and said: "Well, I certainly didn't expect to find some of 'us' in a place like this!" They just laughed and said: "If you think that's something—another one of 'us' is the preacher here!"

Today, that man's family is healed. His marriage is rock solid. He and his wife serve together in the leadership of Serenity Church.

As I had observed before, though, very few people in the recovery community would allow themselves to go so deep in an established "church". Every culture, every denomination, every family has its own language...its own way of expressing things.

I remember my Freshman year in college visiting with a buddy of mine in my dorm room one afternoon and telling him: "I absolutely have to get some laundry done tonight. I'm completely out of clean T-pants." He looked at me like I was speaking Swahili and said: "Clean what?!"..."T-pants. I'm out of clean T-pants"..."What the heck are T-pants?!"...Equally confused, I held up a T-shirt and a pair of BVD briefs, and said: "You know, T-shirts and T-pants!!"

To say the least, I had to graduate and finally leave town before I lived that one down! That's what we called them in our family. It never dawned on me that the whole world didn't call them that. Every culture, every group, every family has its own way of expressing things.

All of us need to hear things in "our language" if it's going to touch and change us. Our denomination, like all groups and cultures, knew how to speak truth to each other. Suddenly, we had a growing group of folks in the room who expressed truth in different ways and with different words. We inevitably hit a wall in trying to absorb them into us.

The Apostle Paul totally understood this principle. It's not the job of the "lost" to adapt to, and learn the language of, the "found". It's our job to speak Christ in their language. To come to them where they are. He put it like this:

"Though I am free and belong to no man, I make myself a slave to everyone, to win as many as possible. To the Jews I became like a Jew, to win the Jews. To those under the law I became like one under the law (though I myself am not under the law), so as to win those under the law. To those not having the law I became like one not having the law (though I am not free from God's law but am under Christ's law), so as to win those not having the law. To the weak I became weak, to win the weak. I have become all things to all men so that by all possible means I might save some. I do all this for the sake of the gospel, that I may share in its blessings." 1 Corinthians 9:19-23 (NIV)

20 years deeply in the recovery community had made something else deeply obvious to me. Recovering people are overwhelmingly "church-ophobic". The "church" has not been a friend to us. Church folks have judged us, condemned us, condescended to us, discarded us. Very few people sitting in those meetings, and in those fellowships, had stories of love and grace dispensed to them by churches. As a result, the millions of people finding God in those circles are not only overwhelmingly unchurched...they recoil from the concept.

We hit that brick wall in our church, too. No matter how hard we tried to love and accept them when they walked through the door—very few would take the risk of walking through that door in the first place. I mentioned the man who asked his sister-in-law to drop him off at church on the way home from the AA meeting. She and her family are deeply a part of Serenity Church today—but she can only laugh about that Sunday morning. She was horrified at the idea of pulling into a church parking lot to let him out—much less walk in herself. As she tells it today, she just kind of slowed down and let him jump out as she sped away!

We had doctrinal, traditional hurdles for the recovering folks, too. These were not "doctrines" in my faith, in the leadership of our church, or most of our members...but they had been in our history and were deeply held traditions today.

One was our music. For many years, as a core "doctrine", our denomination was strictly A Cappella in our worship. I didn't hold that doctrine in my faith, but it was still deeply rooted in the tradition of how we worshipped. I knew that to outsiders coming in it was just quaint, bizarre and irrelevant to them. By the time I was a few days old, I was sitting in church listening to A Cappella worship. It was deep in my DNA, so I "got it". It touched me. To an "outsider" coming in it made no sense at all. That's not the kind of music that touches them. It's not the way they express themselves.

The other giant hurdle was our relationship to women in our church. Other than the act of singing, women were not allowed to open their mouths in our assemblies. If a woman in the children's ministry had an announcement to make, she would have to write it down and find a man to stand up and read it for her. It was that complete. Again, that was not a "doctrine" of MY faith, but it was rooted in practice to the core of us.

The recovery community is blessed with amazing, black-belt, Kung Fu, ninja recovery women whose "experience, strength and hope" are justifiably treasured by those who are walking the walk with them. For us to reach out to those women and say: "Welcome to our church. Now come in, sit down, and keep your mouth shut because you are the wrong gender"... was understandably nonsense to them.

So, no matter how welcoming we tried to be–some of our traditional baggage was always going to drive away many of the very ones we wanted so desperately to reach. We still weren't speaking their language in a way that they could hear it.

TWENTY-TWO

By the Spring of 2005, I was dry, empty, and exhausted. I had been committed now for nearly 30 years to bringing grace and freedom to the people of my roots. Incredibly slow progress was being made. We had climbed over some of those hurdles, but inevitably we'd have to fight those same battles again and again.

I still believed He wanted us to take all the power I had found in those circles that had saved my life—and weave it together with what Christ had intended His church to be. We had a real taste of that dream God had put in me 18 years earlier. That's what it was, though, a "taste". We would always come to a place where we couldn't go any further. The boundaries of our roots and traditions would only let us go so far. I just felt like I was hitting the same brick wall over and over.

A dear friend from one of the fellowships I regularly attended picked up on how drained and tired I really was. One day over lunch he told me he was really concerned about me. He said: "John, you 'sponsor' an army of people. Who looks after you? Who do you take spiritual direction from?"

I honestly didn't have an answer. He told me that he had recently been spending time with a wonderful Christian counselor who had done him a world of good. If he made the arrangements, would I be willing to spend some time with this man? I knew that I needed something to refill my empty bucket. I agreed to meet with him once a week for a while.

Several weeks after we started meeting together, I walked into his office one afternoon for my regular appointment. As soon as I sat down he got to the point. He said: "John, you are dangerously empty. You've poured out of that bucket of yours until there's nothing left to pour. When was the last time you took a sabbatical—some extensive down time to rest, regroup and refill?"

I barely understood that concept. I told him that Kay and I had taken a week of vacation the summer before. He said: "That's not what I'm talking about. You need to unplug, back up, and go away for a while. You need to give God some leisurely time to recharge you. Have you EVER done that?"

Well...no. I asked him how long he was talking about. He said: "What does Scripture say? When Jesus needed to regroup and reconnect with God how long did He take to do that?" I told him that was embarrassing because I had just finished preaching that very principle for 7 weeks. Our church had just gone through the "40 Days of Purpose"... "Would it be 40 days?", I asked him.

"That's what my Bible says. I'm telling you that you need to unplug your computer, turn off your phone, and go away for 40 days to let God rest and refill you. If you don't, I don't think you're going to be okay."

I let him know immediately that was simply out of the question. People need me. Important things won't happen without me. There was simply no way I could let go that long. He said: "Well, the bare minimum that would do you any good is 28 days. I want you to go pray about that and let me know what you decide. If you're not willing to do what I ask you to do, there's really no reason for us to keep meeting. I'll love you just the same, but I'm busy and other people need my time."

I left and wrestled and prayed about that for a few days. He was right. I knew it. But letting go like that was contrary to everything in me. Maybe that's the point: Jump–and let God work out the details. Maybe He could bless a church without me for a while. What a concept! I took a deep breath and decided to do what I was told.

Several nights later, I sat down with the leadership of our church and told them what I had been advised to do. When I finished the story, I told them: "I just don't think I could possibly be away for 40 days! I'm giving real, prayerful, consideration to possibly doing something to recharge for 28 days."

When I finished, my buddy Mark sat back and said: "Let me make sure I'm understanding what you're saying. It took Christ 40 days to 'refill his bucket' but you can do it in 28?".... "No, that's not what I'm saying at all!"... "Oh, yeah, that's exactly what you just said!"

The group was incredibly encouraging and supportive. They understood where I was and agreed with my counselor. They told me to take 40 days to breathe, rest, and recharge. They'd take care of things while I was gone.

Never having done a sabbatical, I had no clue what to do or how to go about this. I sent out an email to several preacher-buddies of mine that I trust, told them my plan, and asked for suggestions about how, and where, to go about this.

The first response I got was later that same day. My friend, Larry, wrote right back and said: "John, this is probably going to sound pretty strange coming from somebody from our background...but I need you to trust me on this. A couple of years ago, I went and spent some time at a Benedictine Monastery in the high desert north of Santa Fe. It's incredibly remote, at the end of a canyon, in one of the most beautiful spots on earth. The Benedictines are a Catholic order who have taken a vow of silence. Their primary "work" is prayer. Part of their ancient tradition is to welcome spiritual pilgrims who need to pull away from the world for a while and spiritually recharge. They keep a 'guesthouse' for that purpose. They'll feed you, house you, and leave you alone to spend time with God. It's one of the holiest places you'll ever be. Go there. Spend some time with them. You'll never be the same."

"Pretty strange" was an understatement! Days of extended "silence" is contrary to my nature–to grossly understate the case. Spiritually recharged, ministered to, by Catholic monks? Really? I had come light years in my journey out of the "us versus you" poison of my roots. I had come to fully understand that "followers of Christ" were found in an incredible variety of fellowships and traditions...but the Catholics?! I had been taught in Sunday School since I was little that Catholicism was the "Great Apostasy". It was the bastardization of Christianity. When the Book of Revelation spoke of the Anti-Christ, it was referring to the Pope. Obviously, I knew better than all of that–but old wiring dies hard.

I trusted Larry, though, and it was time to stretch in new directions. He had included contact information so I emailed them and asked if I could spend a week with them at the Monastery. I got a response right back telling me that they had reserved a room for me and looked forward to my coming. Kay and I made several other plans, including a leisurely drive through New England, and made plans to begin this crazy adventure.

In the week leading up to my departure, I was in my office tying up some loose ends and my secretary buzzed through and said there was a call for me from a man named "Jeff". I picked up the phone. He introduced himself to me and said: "John, I don't think we've ever met each other—but I'm in a world of hurt. I've been calling some preachers that I have respect for, looking for some counsel on what to do next, and I was given your number. I have no idea why."

I told him I couldn't imagine why, either. "Tell me a little bit about what's going on and maybe we can figure it out." He said: "Well, I'm a preacher. I'm married with 3 small children. I'm an alcoholic. I've been hiding my drinking for years. Some folks in our church recently found out—and I was promptly fired."

"Ah", I said, "now we know why you were given MY number!"

We visited for a long time that afternoon. I told him the wisdom that had been given to me when I started the recovery journey. I told him exactly what it would take to start crawling out of that hole. 90 meetings in the next 90 days. Work daily with a good sponsor. Move steadily through "working" those Steps.

I said: "Jeff, this will be almost impossible for you to imagine right now. This afternoon, being discarded by the people you had committed your life to, seems like the worst thing that has ever happened to you. I had to walk all the way through the exact same darkness you're in today...and out the other side... to fully understand what I'm about to say to you. If you will let God fully and completely heal you, if you'll let Him put these pieces back together for you, your real 'ministry' to His people hasn't even started yet. It's all still ahead."

I told him: "Sometimes we get on this merry-go-round that just keeps spinning faster and faster. It's miserable. It makes us sick. But it's the only thing we know to do. We can't let go because we don't know what will happen if we do. We can't jump off. Jumping off a moving object is scary and it hurts. If God really loves us, though, He'll rescue us from that. He'll pick us up and throw us off. That's not painless. It hurts like hell. But now that we're not spinning out of control anymore, He can start to make us well. I look back over my life and I can easily identify the 5 best days of life. Here they are in order: 1) the day I gave my life to Christ and was baptized... 2) the day I married Kay Fry... 3&4) the days my two children were born... 5) the day they fired me from that big church that nearly killed me."

At the end of our visit, I told him: "I'm beginning a 40 day sabbatical next week. Everybody is being told not to call me or contact me during that time. However, my phone will always be in my pocket. Write down this number and if you need to talk to me—use it."

He thanked me for taking time to talk to him. He said he would seriously consider the things I had suggested. He said he would stay in touch. A lot of years of experience told me, though, that he wasn't quite there yet. Jeff had not hit the complete bottom of that pit yet. There is a truth for most of us that we have to "hit bottom". Whatever that is for each of us. We usually don't do the relentless, every day, hard work of recovery until it just hurts too bad NOT TO.

I left for my 40 day spiritual adventure. He didn't call.

TWENTY-THREE

I preached on Sunday, packed and loaded my car, got up Monday morning and drove to Santa Fe. I had no idea what to expect the next morning as I headed north into some of the most beautiful country on God's earth. The road forks in Espanola. West to Chama. East to Taos.

The Brothers had sent me detailed directions. You need them! Taking the west fork, "civilization" began to thin out for the next hour or so. The last thing that qualifies as a "town" is the little village of Abiquiu...best known as the home of Georgia O'Keefe. Her house looks down on you from a bluff as you drive through town. 20 minutes or so north of Abiquiu you only have landmarks to go by. Finally, a tiny sign on the side of the road pointed left and says: "Forest Service Road 151". I turned onto a gravel and dirt road and slowly, carefully, wound my way down that dirt road through the Chama Canyon.

There's simply no way to describe how breath-taking that drive is. Below on my left was the Chama River rushing through the gorge—lined with magnificent old cottonwood trees. Rising up on both sides of the canyon are sheer walls of rock rising hundreds of feet straight up. Pines and aspens look down from the tops of the cliffs.

Finally, after slowly working my way along the winding, narrow, dirt road for most of an hour, I came to another sign: "End of Forest Service Road". I kept going. Over a rise, around a bend, and a hand carved wooden sign simply said: "PEACE. Monastery of Christ in the Desert". Straight ahead, set against the sheer rock of the canyon wall, the monastery faces you like a sentinel welcoming you home. The classic adobe and rough-hewn-beam architecture looks like God designed the canyon around it. The tall bell tower in front of the Monastery church seems to be standing guard protecting something holy.

I was there a week that first trip. It was the first trip of many for me. Every year since then (2005) I have scheduled a week there every June and October. As I write this, I have made my way down that canyon more than a dozen times. My next trip is already scheduled. May God give me many more. There are approximately 25 monks who live their lives there. Their primary reason for being is a full-time ministry of prayer. 7 times a day they ring the big bell in the tower and they silently gather in the little adobe church. They chant the Psalms back and forth to each other as prayer. Guests are invited and welcomed to join them.

The first prayers of the day are at 4:00 AM. One of the monks is assigned by the Abbot as the "Guestmaster". He has special permission to talk to the guests and answer any questions. I asked him once: "So, what's the deal with 4:00 AM?!" His answer: "We believe that the Enemy is strongest in the dark. We rise in the darkest hour of the night and gather to pray against him." I found that logic VERY hard to argue with.

People ask me often what it is that keeps drawing me there. Trip after trip. Year after year. I think I have finally figured out the answer. To be in a place so overwhelmed by some of God's most stunning creation. To be in the fellowship of those godly men who have truly given up everything for Christ. To be surrounded by that concentration of fervent prayer. Obviously, I feel the presence of Christ in a way I don't feel Him any other time or place. But it's more than that. It took me several trips to finally put my finger on it. While I'm there, I feel the ABSENCE of the Enemy. He just has a very hard time getting through the wall of protection that profound.

The rest of that 40 days was everything I needed it to be. I rested. I read. Kay and I spent extended time with people who encourage and refresh us that we just hadn't made time to be with. We flew to New England, rented a car, and just wandered through country that we'd never really experienced. When it came time to return to "reality", I was ready. I had no idea that God had been preparing me for His most significant movement in my life so far.

TWENTY-FOUR

The week I returned to the office I got a call from another stranger. The woman on the other end said: "John, you don't know me. My name is Jennifer. I believe you talked to my husband, Jeff, earlier this summer." I told her that I had and asked how he was doing. She got right to the point: "He nearly died last night."

She went on to explain that he had driven across town the day before in a black-out drunk. He pulled into the parking lot of a fast food place, turned off the ignition, and passed out...in Texas, in August, in the heat of the day, with the windows rolled up. He would have literally cooked in that car if somebody hadn't walked by, saw that something was wrong, and called 9-1-1. It had been a long night in the ER.

She said: "I'm out of answers. I'm running out of hope. I don't know what to do next. Please tell me what to do." I asked her if he was well enough to travel. She thought he was. I told her to put him in the car and bring him to our house as soon as she could arrange it. She left their kids with her folks who lived nearby, and they drove the 3 hours to meet with us. Kay and I sat up until late that night with the two of them telling the story of where we had been, what had happened, and what it was like now.

At the end of that visit, I told them what to do next. Well, "I told them" is not entirely accurate. As I said earlier, I've always had a difficult and uneasy relationship with the principle of

"God told me..." He is given credit for some really ridiculous stuff. Some of the stupidest things ever said and done have followed those words. There are clear times in my life, though, where I know for sure that what comes out of my mouth wasn't from me at all.

I told them to go home and put their house on the market, load up their family, and move NOW to within reach of us. There was simply no way that they were going to win this battle without a strong community of recovering folks tightly wound around them.

That much is pretty much Recovery: 101. Uprooting a family, and moving them across state, is pretty audacious–but getting them surrounded with a healing community right away just makes sense. It was the next part that came from "Somewhere" else.

I told Jeff to sit down the very next day and compile a list of people who love him, people who have been touched and encouraged in some way by his ministry, people who might possibly want to see him eventually restored to doing what God made him to do. Don't judge, I told him. Make the list as long as possible. Anybody, everybody, who has loved you or been invested in God's call on you. Do this first. Do this now. I want that list and their addresses emailed to me within 48 hours. They committed to do both things.

Within 48 hours, I had a lengthy email from Jeff with a long list of names and addresses. In those same two days, I had already composed a letter to go out to all those folks.

I told them briefly what was happening. I told them that I knew what it was like to fight this kind of life-and-death battle while worrying about how I was going to feed my family. Nearly 20 years earlier, Kay and I had been right where they were. The Enemy has been clever and successful in sidelining too many gifted warriors who never had the time or the opportunity to be lifted back up, and put back into service, after they had fallen. It was time to draw a line in the sand and tell him that he couldn't have this one. We needed about a year to provide the kind of healing that it would take to prepare him for a lifetime of victory, one day at a time, in this deadly struggle that had nearly killed him.

How could they help? Help feed his family for those months while he fought this battle with some strong help. Put a roof over their heads. Take care of them temporarily while he healed, and was given the tools, that this new way of living his life would require. Please prayerfully consider sending financial support to keep his family afloat for the next few months. Above all, hold them up in prayer. Constantly hold them up to the One who will heal them and put their pieces in place.

We could not have imagined the response. Almost immediately, replies began to flood in. Most included checks large and small. Many promised regular financial support as long as necessary. All of them expressed deep love and extraordinary grace for Jeff, Jennifer, and their family. They told story after story of the ways their lives had been touched by them. They told of Jeff's incredible gift for preaching that was so obviously from God.

God stepped in again and they sold their house almost immediately. Again–and Jennifer found a teaching job with a local school district. They were with us in a matter of weeks.

Understanding that this was a spiritual and physical sickness that can effect the family even more painfully than the addict or alcoholic, a group of our "black-belt" recovering women formed a tight circle around Jennifer to hold her up and walk her through her own recovery. They committed to stay in touch with her daily with whatever she needed to kick-start her healing. I've said countless times that the ones who love us have a struggle every bit as deep, or deeper, than ours. We can anesthetize ours. You just have to helplessly hurt. That recovery can be the toughest of all.

I asked one of our guys with many years of recovery, and sponsoring other men in recovery, to serve as Jeff's initial sponsor and begin walking him through the steps. That began before they finished unpacking. He immediately began his 90-in-90.

The first piece of the puzzle, though, I had put in place while we waited for them to arrive. I had contacted the Monastery and scheduled 2 weeks for him in their guesthouse.

Jeff and I sat down to discuss the plan for his healing. I told him that he would be leaving right away for the "desert". He was in desperate need of spiritual and emotional "de-tox". There is simply no place on earth that can provide that better. I prepared him as best I could for what to expect. The Monastery is over an hour's drive to the nearest electric service or cell phone signal. The guesthouse is a classic "L"-shaped adobe building with two long porches that look out across the canyon. They call the rooms "cells". Not a bad description! Concrete floors, adobe walls, a little handmade desk and chair and a bed.

The monks provide 3 meals a day for their guests and the opportunity to join their prayers and share their life with them. The great gift and power of all of that, though, is the opportunity to not only talk to God—but to sit and listen. It's unstructured time to read, pray, hike through that gorgeous canyon...and just "be", with no pressure, no expectations, and almost vacuum quiet. I told him he'd be there for 14 days. The women ministering to Jennifer and the kids guaranteed that they'd be well taken care of while he was gone. He packed, loaded up his car, and headed 650 miles west for whatever it was that God wanted to accomplish with him there. God has been taking His people into the desert to rebuild, reshape, and prepare them since the beginning of time. Most notably...his own Son.

A week later, I saw Jennifer at church on Sunday. I walked over, hugged her, and asked if everything was okay with Jeff gone. She said that she and the kids were being well taken care of by her "crew".

"I guess you know", she said, "that he'll be back home tonight." To say the least, that was news to me: "No, he's there for 2 weeks. He won't be home until this time next week."

"Oh, he called me this morning from Cline's Corners. He said it had been a wonderful experience—but he thought he had what he went there for and was coming on home."

I said: "When he gets home tonight, please tell him not to unpack and to be at my door first thing tomorrow morning!"

The first thing the next morning Jeff arrived at my door. He immediately launched into a speech that he'd obviously had a lot of miles to rehearse. It was a great experience. He was glad that he went. He felt really rested. God had really worked on him. He thought he had gotten everything he went there to get...

That's when I interrupted the speech: "Here's the thing, Jeff, you don't get to think right now. Your best thinking very nearly killed you. You're going to learn how to think healthy and well—but you're not there today. In the meantime, some of us are doing some thinking for you...and you need to do what we ask you to do."

He stood there for a moment while all the pieces fell into place and then asked me: "So, you want me to go back?".... "I do. I want you to stay the two weeks we agreed to"... "Would it be alright if I stayed tonight, did some laundry, spent a little time with my kids, and head out early tomorrow morning?"... "Absolutely"... "Then that's what I'll do"... and he walked out my door, got in his car, and drove off.

Early the next morning, Jeff started the 1300 mile round-trip back to the place he had just left. That's when I knew he had what it took to win this battle, and there was great hope for him.

This is a battle that's all or nothing. On page 58 of the "Big Book" of Alcoholics Anonymous", in the opening of the chapter, "How It Works", are words that are read to open every meeting around the world...

"If you have decided you want what we have and are willing to go to any length to get it—then you are ready to take certain steps. At some of these we balked. We thought we could find an easier, softer way. But we could not. With all the earnestness at our command, we beg of you to be fearless and thorough from the very start....Some of us have tried to hold on to our old ideas and the result was nil until we let go absolutely...Half measures availed us nothing. We stood at the turning point. We asked His protection and care with complete abandon."

The lesson of that day was that "half measures" don't bring us half of it, or some of it, or a little of it. "Half measures availed us nothing."

As our Higher Power said it even better: "In the same way, any of you who does not give up everything he has cannot be my disciple". Luke 14:33 (NIV)

TWENTY-FIVE

That Fall was one of the sweetest times of my life. The hurting and broken continued to pour in. The Overcomers group that had started in my office with 4 of us–consistently had 10 times that many crammed into that same space. Jeff was working feverishly to jump-start a life in recovery and sobriety. I went back to the Monastery that October. In the quiet stillness of the Chama Canyon, I could see clearly what had been swirling around me. I was overwhelmed with the obvious fact that God was unfolding something new and powerful.

As the Holidays approached, Kay and I made plans to take a little breather together. To say the least, that time of the year is not exactly "downtime" for a pastor. She and I traditionally schedule a week away right after Christmas. We'll book a B&B... or just take some leisurely day trips. Lots of "after Christmas sales" get some careful attention from us that week. Kay will usually have most of next year's Christmas shopping done by New Year's.

One thing that had really struck me in all of those letters we had received in response to our request for support for Jeff's family...was the incredible passion of people's descriptions of his preaching. Over and over and over I heard what an extraordinary "gift" of preaching he had been given and what a tragic waste it would be to lose it.

Jeff was already a different man than the one I had met just a few months earlier. He was clear-eyed and hopeful with 4 months of sobriety. We'd had at least a dozen conversations during those months where he tossed around whether he'd ever preach again. Was he even supposed to preach? Was that what God intended for him? What other options would there be to make a living and support his family?

As the Holidays approached, I asked him over lunch one day if he thought he might be ready to take a first step back into a pulpit. It had been since back in the Spring when his church had fired him. In a time when I had felt so "disgraced", some dear brothers had put me in their pulpits. It had made such a difference for me. How did he feel about speaking for God like that again? I told him that Kay and I would be away for a few days around New Years. Would he consider filling in for me that Sunday?

I wish I had a film clip of that conversation and his response! It was like a switch had been flipped and his whole body beamed. Sure...absolutely...I'd love to...are you sure I'm ready?! I assured him that he was. I told him to start preparing.

On Sundays off like that, I always enjoyed dropping in and just "attending" a church service somewhere new, get a fresh perspective, hear somebody else preach. That Sunday, though, I felt a deep need to hear for myself what was coming out of our pulpit. We didn't tell anybody that we'd be there. We sneaked in a few minutes after the service started and sat as inconspicuously as possible on the back row.

When Jeff stepped up to preach, for just a few moments he seemed to hesitate a little while he got his bearings—and then the floodgate blew open. Oh my, did that boy PREACH. I just sat there spellbound and mesmerized while the Spirit literally blew out of him.

When the service concluded, Jeff was standing at the front of the sanctuary. I began to make my way through through the crowd toward him. Halfway there I bumped into Jennifer. I gave her a bear hug, looked her square in the eyes, and said: "People kept telling me—but there's no way I could have imagined what I just witnessed." She just beamed and said, "go tell him that."

When I finally reached Jeff, I hugged him hard, got right in his face, and said: "Listen to me carefully. You and I have had many conversations on the topic: 'Am I supposed to preach?' Those conversations are over. Most people can go to school and be taught how to write, prepare, and deliver a nice lesson. Only a relative handful are given the Spirit Gift of proclamation. I just saw the Spirit move through one of that handful. If you are given the "Gift", you don't get to choose. God expects, requires, you to use it."

I knew as I walked out to the parking lot that life would never be the same. I finally had the help I needed to keep an old promise. It was time for SERENITY CHURCH....

TWENTY-SIX

The next couple of weeks I prayed relentlessly about it and spent hours discussing it with Kay and a handful of folks that I trusted to tell me the truth. I knew that this would be one of the biggest commitments of my life. If I jumped here and took the people I love with me, there were a thousand ways to fail and fall. I understood the principle—but I had no clue what the details of starting a whole new spiritual movement looked like.

After a couple of weeks of alternating thrill and terror, I sat down with the rest of the leadership of our church and told them what I was hearing, and had known, for a long time:

...There are literally millions of people in the recovery community, deeply committed to God and fellowship with His people, who are truly "churchaphobic". They desperately need Christ but have been wounded and discarded by "Christians". The vast majority are "unchurched". There are many thousands of those people within minutes us.

...Expecting them to adapt to us, to wade through our traditions and eccentricities, to find Christ wasn't working and wasn't right. (Phil. 3:4-7)

...Our services had a very limited ability to speak to them. Two significant obstacles were our style of music and our complete silencing of our women.

...They need to hear Christ spoken in the same language as the meeting they sat in the night before. Fortunately, God had assembled a nucleus of us who are fluently bi-lingual. Dozens of us in our fellowship speak fluent Church and fluent Recovery.

...It was equally wrong to stop ministering to our established congregation in the way that they hear, speak, are touched, and understand. The only way to truly reach both is to provide two times, two venues, for fellowship and worship where each "language" is heard and understood.

...Our building was regularly locked and dark on Saturday nights. That seemed to be the perfect time to begin something radical and new to reach those who are not being reached. My experience with the recovery community is that they really don't have a major problem with Sunday morning. Saturday nights? Now, that's another issue! They have a deep need to be some place happy, healthy, and encouraging at the very same time that we had an empty place that should be used.

...God had brought us exactly the help that we needed to launch this new thing. We would essentially have 2 churches meeting under one roof. It was all I could do to pastor one. We had assumed that God brought Jeff and his family to us so that we could help them. Maybe an equal reason was that He knew we needed their help. We had an unused, Spirit-gifted, preacher sitting in our pews who was rapidly becoming fluent in all things "recovery".

The response from the entire leadership team was instantaneous and excited. Really, the one question was: "How quickly can we start this up?!" I had assumed that I would have to convince them and drag them along. The first thing I had to do was to "tap the brakes"!

There were still the pesky little problems of figuring out what this looks like, how it works, getting the word out to the people we're trying to reach, coming up with music and musicians radically different than anything we had ever done...and a host of other hurdles and questions we hadn't even thought of yet.

This was January. We did need to set a launch date so that we had a target to shoot for. After some serious prayer and discussion, we put the pin on the calendar and committed to the Saturday night of Pentecost weekend...June 3, 2006. God has a history of great "beginnings" on Pentecost! There were a LOT of things that needed to happen in just a little over 4 months.

The first thing, was to share this vision with our entire church. I didn't know exactly what the response would be—but I was hopeful. By this time, we had been a part of them for almost 10 years. For almost a decade I had relentlessly preached grace, spiritual freedom, and a non-denominational-Jesus to them. I thought that they would be ready to stretch in a totally new direction. With the scores of recovery folks that had been filling our pews in recent months...they would have a face-to-face understanding of the "community" we were talking about.

I stood up the following Sunday morning and shared the plan and the vision with the church. I made all the points I had made with the leadership earlier that week. The two points that I was afraid would be potential "land mines" were the music and the equality of women. Both of these were deeply rooted "doctrinal" points in the tradition we came from. I thought that after all these years we had grown past all of that. We'd see.

As I summed it all up, I assured them that none of this would affect them at all unless they chose to be involved with us on

Saturday nights. Sunday morning assemblies would look just like they always had. This is what they had come here for. We wouldn't take this away from them. This was just another way, at another time, to reach another group of people for Christ who were not being reached. I understood that there might be some additional questions. If anybody wanted to meet with me and discuss any of this, I'd be in my office the following night at 7:00 and would be happy to discuss any questions they may have.

I was not prepared for the buzz-saw I walked into on Monday night. I thought a couple of folks might stop by. 40 people crammed into my office. The mood was some combination of anger, fear, and confusion. For three solid hours I sat on the firing line while all of that was directed at me. It wasn't pretty.

I had assumed the Big Issue was going to be the "praise band". A Cappella worship had been our major, most obvious, distinctive for generations. It had historically been a doctrinal line-in-the-sand that had separated "true believers" from the apostate. That concept was barely mentioned that night–or in the weeks and months to come.

The Big Issue was allowing women to talk to God, and share their faith, out loud in that building. The overwhelming majority of the opposition was coming from my sisters in the room. That part didn't surprise me.

I kept explaining that if that was offensive to them they were not expected to be a part it. This is a separate thing–on another day. Their Sunday morning worship experience would look just like it always had. That didn't help. As one woman summed it up loudly: "I will not raise my daughters in a place where women are not kept silent whatever the day of the week."

We'll pause for a moment here and let you soak up the irony...

The issue that came in right behind it was the fear of encouraging too many of "those people" to come to "our place". Here's where the fear pretty much matched the anger. "What do we know about 'those people' really?... Are they dangerous?... Will our children be safe?... Could we require them to undergo background checks?... Will they mess up our building?..."

After hours of this, there was not much left to say. We dismissed and I limped home.

Over the next day or two I relayed the details of the meeting to the rest of our leadership. To their great credit they didn't budge. This was right. Christ would be pleased with it. We're going to do it. By the time summer arrived and God birthed this new thing nearly 1/4 of our church had left.

TWENTY-SEVEN

The key to our timing, the trigger that had set all of this in motion, was Jeff being there to help. Spirit-powered preaching—spoken in the language, and through the filter, of the recovery community—was critical to reaching who we were trying to reach. Pastoring what was now a very troubled suburban church of the denomination of my roots was more than a full-time job. Producing additional sermons each week spoken to a people, and in a language, very different from Sunday morning would be more of me than I had to give.

We had asked people to financially support Jeff and his family for one year. They had responded overwhelmingly and done just that. That time would be coming to a close at the end of the summer. We didn't know what the future held—but we couldn't plan on Jeff's full-time attention after that. I sat down with him and challenged him to be the preacher for Serenity Church for our kick-off summer. We'd call it the "Summer of Serenity". He would preach the first twelve weeks—preaching each of the 12-Steps through the perspective of Scripture (still available on our website!). I would pick it up in the Fall and preach them again. He was thrilled and more than ready to take on that challenge.

Speaking of "challenges", everything else was up for grabs. We had no idea what this was supposed to look like. The first, and most uncomfortable, unknown for me was the music for this brand new thing. I understood that the folks we were trying to touch were not going to be touched by a solid diet of centuries-old hymns. A steady stream of A Cappella would just seem strange to them. We needed a gifted, high-energy praise band. Never having preached for a church that had so much as a piano in the room, I had no idea how to start to make that happen.

Less than a month after we made our announcement, two young guys in their 20s strolled into my office one day and the oldest one introduced them: "I'm Jason and this is my brother, Jered. I sing, play the guitar, and write some Christian praise music. Jered plays the drums. We've heard that you're about to do something really cool here and we were just wondering if you could use some help?"

I knew that God had led them to my door—but I had no idea what a gift he had dropped in our laps. Jason immediately became the Worship Leader for Serenity Church...and is to this day. As I said, my experience is limited but I've had hundreds of people tell me through the years that he is, without a doubt, one of the most gifted leaders they've ever worshipped with. I can't imagine God using anybody more powerfully.

Immediately on the heels of that introduction, incredibly gifted musicians began to come out of the woodwork. The recovery community is full of talented musicians with nowhere to point those talents. When you have those abilities and can no longer take them to the bars and honky-tonks, where can you go to use them? My fear had been that we would have nobody to help us make music. The "problem" we had by our first service was how to fit them all on the stage!

Within a month of announcing our plans, we took a special contribution at our church on Sunday morning to help with the expenses of the materials we'd need—and to help us "get the word out". We were thrilled and humbled when more than $20,000 came in that morning to help us get started. We quickly formed a team of our recovering folks to make the decisions and complete the projects on an ever-growing list.

First on the list: how do we let the people that we're trying to reach know that we're here? We didn't have a clue where to start. There were 6 million people within an hour of us. Tens of thousands of them are people in the recovery community who are desperately searching for more information and a deeper relationship with the "Higher Power". How could we reach them? How do you communicate with an invisible, anonymous community of people? In a media market that large, we couldn't begin to afford classic advertising in any traditional sense.

That doesn't mean that we didn't try. Our single biggest financial investment in those early weeks was to purchase some of the slides that flash on the screen at local movie theaters before the previews start. We just knew that thousands would get the word that way. To my knowledge, not a single person ever found their way to us because they saw a slide on a screen 20 minutes before their movie started.

My friend Sherman designed a wonderful logo for us. We had hundreds of T-shirts printed with our logo and our web address and gave them to anybody who would wear one. It's understandably, and correctly, inappropriate to discuss your church in any of the meetings of the fellowships we were part of. I totally understand that principle and defend it. However...if you happened to be wearing a shirt that caused somebody to ask you questions after the meeting, out on the parking lot, well, we're not going to turn down that opportunity! That turned out to be one of our most effective tools to open doors to tell people about ourselves.

By a Divine "coincidence" I was invited to speak that Spring to a conference of leaders of Christian recovery groups from all over our area. I shared our vision with them and begged them to come and help us–at least through the first weeks and help us get our feet on the ground. They excitedly committed to do that...and did. Although none of them would be part of us for the long haul–their presence in those first weeks made all the difference.

We put together bags of stuff that would explain us, and help spread the word, to give to everyone who walked through our door. There were pamphlets with information about us, a pen with our logo on it, a T-shirt, a Bible with a sticker on the cover with our logo and web address. We refer to it as the "Sereni-bag of Sereni-swag". Things have been added and subtracted from it over the years–but the purpose is to always have something with us that we can hand to whomever God leads us to. That has been incredibly effective.

The bags also include a "Serenity Church" medallion that was one of our major, and best, investments. The recovery community marks milestones and treasures the "medallions" given to members as we walk the journey. Our Overcomers Fellowship had been ordering, from our beginning, from Wendells in Minnesota–one the largest mints/suppliers of recovery coins and medallions in the world. We contacted them and made arrangements for them to mint bronze medallions especially for us. One side is engraved with the Serenity Prayer. The other side is engraved with our logo, our slogan "Power For The Powerless", and our web address: www.serenitychurch.net Everyone who visits us for the first time is given one of those medallions in their welcome bag. We carry them in our pocket for opportunities that come up to point people our direction.

Everything points someone curious to our website. I just can't over-stress the importance of an informative, up-to-date website...that truly reflects who, what, and where we are. I have a buddy who says that "Serenity Church is a Movement and a website". He's not far off on that. For reasons that I'll explain in detail later, it's highly unlikely that we'll ever be the owners of a "church building". Our presence is spread all over several cities all during the week. The folks who are a regular, faithful part of us often live nearly 100 miles apart. Our Overcomers Fellowship meets during the week in several different cities—over an hour apart. How do people find us? The website. It tells you where, when, and how, to find us. All of our messages can be listened to and downloaded there. It's the connecting link between the members of our Family. It keeps us updated on what's going on. It is truly our presence and connecting link through the week.

The months leading up to our "birthing" of this new thing for God flew by way too fast. All of the stuff was ordered and delivered. The website was up and running. We had prayerfully pieced together what our assemblies should include and look like. The band had been rehearsing and preparing for months.

Now seemed the perfect time to panic and I was right on the edge of exactly that. Was I crazy? What was I thinking? Who was I to dare something this outlandish? I know me. I know what I am. I know all that I'm NOT. Who was I to think that God would use the likes of me...of us...to do a whole new thing for Him? It had rocked the foundations of the church that I had served and loved for a decade. Scores of people I loved, and had poured my life into, had walked out of my life rather than be any part of this thing. The church I served was hemorrhaging. This new thing was just a dream. Was I out of my mind? Had I heard Him right?

Two weeks before we launched, I pulled loose and drove that long drive to spend several days at the Monastery. I absolutely did not have time to do that. I also understood that I didn't have time NOT TO. I needed silence to wrestle with God one more time before we jumped.

I've kept a journal of every visit I've made to that sweet place. I recently re-read the frantic words I wrote that week:

"May 24, 2006. I so desperately needed to be here. Being "in labor" since February, working furiously to birth Serenity Church, has been a roller coaster of giddy high and heart-breaking low... so much joy and so much sadness...so much anticipation and so much fear. I'm writing this Wed. morning–10 days from June 3rd. Lord, did I hear you right? Is this your will? Will you bring your broken ones to us for the dispensing of grace and healing? I have never believed more deeply that I heard you more clearly. Lord, help my unbelief. Launch a revolution of healing...a tidal wave of spiritual reawakening. Please send your Spirit down on us this Pentecost. Light that fire again! Send us salvaged souls, workers, resources, whatever money is genuinely needed. Keep the Enemy away from us. Give us clear, united, vision. Protect us. Empower us...LORD, HELP MY UNBELIEF!!!"

The week I got home was a frenzy of last minute details...and then it was time. Saturday, June 3rd, 2006...the night before Pentecost. It felt like my whole life had led up to this moment. A lifetime looking for freedom and the answers. Nearly 20 years of healing and dreaming. 5 months of frantic preparation. The week leading up to this moment spent at the Monastery in the desert–begging God to bless this new thing–to show up and bring His people. It all came down to this moment, Saturday night, June 3rd...the night before Pentecost.

Those of us that God had called, and brought together, to "birth this baby" had thought about little else these last few weeks. Had we done everything we could do? Was there somebody else we should have talked to? Were all the details in place? We all started showing up hours early. The band went through the music one more time. Jeff was in his little office pacing and mumbling to himself–going over and over the words he'd been preparing for weeks. The welcome crew had the "welcome bags" full, and the t-shirts all folded, lined up and ready.

At around 6:00 we all gathered up in a circle and asked God one more time to bless this new thing. Please, God, send your Spirit tonight like you did that other Pentecost. Bring the people...the broken, the hurting, the lost, the discouraged...please bring them here. Use us to dispense your hope and healing. Do again here, tonight, what you have done for all of us. Please give us this "front row seat" to watch you do what you do.

We were thrilled. We were hopeful. We were anxious. We were ready. Around 6:30 they began to come. First they trickled in...and then they poured in. Motorcycles rumbled into the parking lot. The cars stacked up in the driveway. People who had always believed they didn't belong in a place like this walked through the door to see if it was true. You could see it in their eyes. Is this for real? Do I actually belong here? There was a roar of excitement as the room filled up. People who didn't know each other met. Old friends noisily reunited. Lots of hugging. Lots of laughing.

At straight up 7:00 the screens overhead lit up with a digital countdown. 5 minutes to go. The music thumped. The numbers flashing on the screen worked their way down...:05, :04, :03, :02, :01..."WELCOME TO SERENITY CHURCH!!" The crowd roared! God began a whole new thing. None of us would ever be the same. Saturday night, June 3rd...the night before Pentecost.

TWENTY-EIGHT

That first night flew by in a blur. There were over 200 people that night. The excitement in that room was so thick you could have cut it with a knife. Some of the "logistics" worked exactly as we had planned and hoped. Others we scrapped and rearranged on the fly.

Jeff stood up to preach and was literally on fire. The blending of recovery language and Scripture...truth they knew and truth they didn't...was perfect. The Spirit literally took him over.

Most of us, including Jeff, were wearing shorts and flip-flops that night. In his excitement he kicked off his flip-flops as he started to preach. Over the next few days several people kidded him about it. He was genuinely embarrassed. The next time we visited he said: "John, I can't believe I preached barefoot—I promise I'll never do that again!"

"Oh, yes you will", I told him, "every family needs traditions and that's now one of ours. God told Moses to take off his shoes... he was on holy ground. This is a very holy thing we get to do. Barefoot is probably the only appropriate way to do it."

Every sermon preached at Serenity Church since that night has come from a barefoot preacher. We're on holy ground!

We knew that a lot of the folks in the room that night were not going to be part of this for the long haul. Many were friends and loved ones who had specifically come to encourage us on that first night.

I didn't have time to analyze what had happened that night because I had a whole different group to pastor the next morning. With very little sleep I got up early the next morning and plowed though another full day of pastoring and preaching...to a very different group...in a very different way.

Over the next week we met often to debrief what had happened, what worked and what didn't, what to subtract and what to add. The following Saturday we all got there hours early and went through all of that preparing again. It was a wonderful night of real joy and grace—with about half as many people. There were new folks there for the first time who are still with us today. We have never had a service of Serenity Church that God has not brought new people into the room for the first time.

By the end of the first month, we had settled in consistently to around 50-60 people. I'd be lying if I told you that there was not a part of me that was a little bit discouraged by that small number in that big room. It's hardwired into preachers to judge the success of what we're trying to do for God by the "head count" in the room.

Offsetting that, though, was the sheer, big-eyed, gratitude of the people in that room. I would look across that room into the faces of people who would never find a place in a tidy, traditional, suburban church. They belonged here. These were their people. They felt it. They knew it.

Some of the most encouraging words for me that summer came in a conversation with a dear brother who was pastoring a church of thousands. He asked me to tell him all about Serenity

Church and what God was doing. I gave him a detailed account of where we were and what was happening.

When I finished, he said to me: "John, I have to be honest with you here—I'm really, really, jealous. What you are doing is the real thing. It's what Christ intended for it to be. Christ doesn't need any more fresh-scrubbed suburban churches. What He's looking for are outposts for the Kingdom."

No words spoken to me in this adventure have encouraged me more or made more sense. Outposts for the Kingdom. Rescue stations. Spiritual emergency rooms and triage units. Places where dying people can go and learn how to live. All churches have a revolving door of some kind. Ours more than most. God leads people in every week to learn how not to die. Some will stay on for the journey with us. Many will not. Some will take the tools we give them and use them in other places.

Although God has grown our numbers over the years since then—that's still not the point. I tell our folks regularly that we will never be a church who can put together a nice pictorial directory and have it make sense a year later. Does the patient roster in the Emergency Room of your local hospital look the same this time next year? Hopefully not!

We constantly face the classic choice—are we a "movement" or a "monument"? A monument is all about holding on to where we come from. Monument churches carefully tend "membership rosters", build walls, and carefully hold what "belongs" to them in. There's not even a whisper of a suggestion of our fiercely defended "local church membership" principle in Scripture. Christ's followers are by definition a movement...coming together to recharge and encourage each other...and then spreading out wherever He needs us to reproduce what He's done for us.

We quickly learned that "results" are not only impossible to define, particularly with the deeply broken folks that God was leading to us, they're also none of our business! That whole arrogant madness of "which preacher has the most impressive results" was already erupting when the preachers involved were the Apostles. Paul was flabbergasted to hear that his "results" were being compared to his friend Apollos. He wanted to put a stop to that foolishness immediately. All of us bring the gift we've been given, make it available to God, and then He will do with it whatever He chooses. As Paul summed it up:

"What, after all, is Apollos? And what is Paul? Only servants, through whom you came to believe—as the Lord has assigned to each his task. I planted the seed, Apollos watered it, but God made it grow. So neither he who plants nor he who waters is anything, but only God, who makes things grow. The man who plants and the man who waters have one purpose, and each will be rewarded according to his own labor. For we are God's fellow workers; you are God's field, God's building." 1 Corinthians 3:5-9 (NIV)

Wouldn't you love to see a graph of Jesus' "membership roster" during his personal preaching ministry? He started with a handful, built a following of thousands, and by the time he brought His ministry to the cross there were only 3 in attendance that day.

We learned in those early months that if you're going to give yourself to the messy, the deeply broken, and the "least of these"...prepare to have your heart broken. Life lived in trenches this deep is not for the squeamish.

In those early weeks, one of those that God brought to us immediately moved into the heart of us. Billy was an alcoholic who wanted sobriety so desperately. I began to meet with him weekly to help him walk through the steps. He honored me deeply by trusting me to be the one who heard his "5th Step". Just a few days later I baptized him into our Family. A few days following that–he led our communion service. There were very few dry eyes in the room that night.

What we didn't know that night was that there had been a hold up with his doctor and his pharmacy getting his prescription refilled for the anti-depressants that he relied on to keep functioning. He couldn't pick up his prescription until Tuesday. As he felt himself slide back into that old, familiar, dark pit he panicked and did what he knew to do...he self-medicated with alcohol.

Tuesday finally came and he headed for the pharmacy–drunk. Halfway there he flipped his car and died instantly.

In a matter of weeks I had heard his searching and fearless moral inventory, baptized him, received Holy Communion from him...and preached his funeral.

Was all of that a waste? Was it a loss? Hardly. Billy wound up his time here knowing Christ. Christ was with him. That alone would make everything we're trying to do, and be, much more than worth it.

The struggles in the lives of the people that God brings to us are not simple or casual. They come to us desperately trying to not die. It takes repeated tries for the vast majority of us to finally start to experience the miracle. "Relapsing" is not a surprise. Relapsing is what we naturally do. No one who walks through the door into our fellowship has stumbled or screwed-up for the last time. The point is not whether we fall or not. The whole point is: do we we keep letting Him pick us back up.

We stand at a constantly revolving door. Some come in and stay for the journey with us. Some walk back out that door many times before they're finally ready to stay and let the miracle happen. Many of them will walk back out and we'll never see them again.

Our role in all of that is not complicated. We always stand there with our arms open and our hand out ready to help them climb out of that pit again. We plant. We water. It's Someone else's job to change the lives and "make it grow".

TWENTY-NINE

That first summer flew by. We kept fine-tuning what we were doing, and how we were doing it, literally every week. New folks came, and others disappeared, every week. Jeff unfolded one of the Steps for us each week weaving Scripture and recovery literature and language together beautifully. As the series began to wind up and the "Summer of Serenity" was nearing an end, it was time to seriously consider: "What's next"?

The struggle continued at that sweet church that we had served for so many years. A large percentage of them simply could not adjust to our not only allowing, but pursuing, "those people". They didn't understand them. The were uncomfortable about this new thing going on in their home. The vast majority never attended a service of Serenity Church. They didn't understand what was happening there on Saturday night—but they knew it was something radically different than what they understood and were comfortable with. A few excitedly helped and supported us. Some just stayed confused and unhappy. Many more simply left.

Our church finances reflected all of that. By September it became painfully obvious that we could no longer afford all of our remaining staff. Somebody would have to be removed from our congregation's payroll. There were only two salaries that would make that difference. It was either me or our Youth Minister. I had stated publicly, repeatedly, that if that decision had to be made it would be me. I was the shepherd. Scripture is clear that when sacrifice comes–the shepherd sacrifices first. Our Youth Minister was incredibly gifted. The loss to our kids would be deeply damaging.

Jeff was actively preparing for the next chapter of his family's life. He felt deeply called to pursue an officer commission as a U. S. Air Force Chaplain. That long process was well underway. Within months he would receive his commission and his family would be moving to Arkansas.

It was time for me to step up to preach for Serenity Church. In early September I added that to my life and schedule. I knew immediately that this was not going to work.

A couple of weeks later, Kay and I were on our usual, late-night walk around the neighborhood. I mentioned earlier that we have always solved most of life's problems on long walks around the neighborhood. This one would change everything for us. It's another one of those moments in life that is permanently freeze-framed in my mind. I remember what street we were on, what corner we were coming to, the feel of the air that night.

Trying to start a frightening conversation off lightly, I said: "Honey, you and I both know that I'm a mathematical nincom-poop–but, fortunately, you're a professional mathematician. Here's my problem: I'm giving about 3/4 of me to pastoring and leading a confused and very troubled suburban church with a large, and incredibly painful, identity crisis. At the same time, I'm giving about 3/4 of me to being a part of the birthing of something truly new for God–unlike anything else that I know of. Here's my question: Do two 3/4s add up?"

The "lightness" of that moment stopped there. "No", she said, "it doesn't. It's actually way more of you than you have to give."

"What's killing me", I told her, "is that I'm not giving all of me to anything."

She didn't hesitate: "You're right. You're going to have to do one or the other. You're going to have to choose—and I'm not going to waste time in this conversation by asking you where your heart is. We both know that answer."

Suddenly, the reality of what we were saying hit me right in the gut—followed by a jolt of real fear. "You know what this means, don't you? We've spent our entire married life comfortably provided for by a stable church payroll. That's what pays our bills. That's what pays the mortgage on that beautiful house we live in...and the cars we drive...and the clothes we wear.

"I know what these folks drop into those green baskets that we pass at the end of the services at Serenity Church. They used to put a dollar in the basket at each meeting at their 'home group'... but now, they're really supporting their recovery—they're putting in $2. But this is different, this is their CHURCH, they'll put in $5 there.

"These folks have no concept of 'tithing'. I totally understand that tithing and 'stewardship' of our finances are incredibly Biblical themes. The problem in this case, though, is that in most cases we have so little time to get the most urgent message to the folks who need it. People walk through that door every Saturday night literally dying. They have a deep ingrained mistrust of all things 'church'. They assume that WE want something from THEM. I may only have one shot to say the words that will help them not die this week. I'm just not going to take that shot asking for their wallets—and meeting them with a series on 'tithing'. If we give our whole lives to this new thing I have no idea how we're going to pay our bills and live in that house."

She didn't hesitate for a second. "Well, the point is—it's what you're supposed to do. We both know that. I don't have to live in that nice house. It's just the two of us. Our kids are grown, happily and well married, and are taking care of themselves. I can live anywhere. All I'd ask is that it be within driving distance of the High School so I can get there and teach Algebra. You really don't have a choice—it's what you're supposed to do."

Two weeks later, I stood up on Sunday morning and told those folks how desperately I love them. I told them that 10 years with them, the privilege of shepherding that flock, had been one of the sweetest chapters of my life. I explained again that God had clearly called me to be part of this new thing for Him. It would take everything in me and then some. I told them that one salary needed to come off the payroll. As I had promised, that would be me. This new thing would need my full attention. I asked them to please understand that I truly believed I was following God's direction for the next chapter of my life.

At the end of that day, Kay and I had essentially jumped off a cliff with no visible parachute. At the same time, this meant that we were no longer part of the denomination that generations of our families had been born into—that we had both been part of since birth. There's no middle ground. You're either in that system or you're not. It was one of the most exhilarating, purely terrifying moments of our lives.

THIRTY

Suddenly, I was the pastor of a church with no established leadership, no tax status, no permanent home, no bank account... basically nothing that we take for granted when we "do church". Immediately, my friend David pulled along beside me—and has never left.

David and I met each other in a recovery group meeting in Dallas years earlier. We became life-friends immediately. He was in the middle of an imploding marriage and an ugly divorce. Even though he lived a considerable distance away—he began to drive regularly to the church that I pastored. In no time, he was a faithful worker in several of our ministries. Several years later, he met an amazing Christian woman. He and Trena were married by the pond in our back yard.

When Serenity Church was being birthed, they were relentless workers in every piece of it. When I resigned everything that I knew and jumped without that "visible parachute", they grabbed our hands and refused to let us fall. David looked me in the eye and assured me that we had heard right. He promised that Kay and I would not do without because of this decision. He meant it. He is by no means a wealthy man—but during those early months he personally saw to it that we lacked for nothing we needed.

It was right in the middle of this storm that we came face to face with a small group of folks who had been there all along.

They would change our lives and make all the difference in the next chapter of Serenity Church.

Jason, our worship leader on Saturday nights, served the same role on Sunday mornings for a little storefront church down the street. They had been at one time a large, influential church in town. Years of fussing, fighting, and splitting had dwindled them down to a sweet, faithful remnant who stayed faithful through all of those storms. They believed God had not released them from His call to their church. When they could no longer pay for their building they sold it, took the proceeds, and had rented a variety of places from which they desperately tried to serve and be of use. They had hired a young man as their pastor and tried to do a truly new thing for God in our community. He and I had become friends. He was the one who told Jason about us and sent him our way. They came our first night to see what we were about. They kept coming. In that first summer, they had come to us and asked if they could rent space in our building for their Sunday services. We quickly agreed.

Serenity Church was now renting space in that same building. We woke up one day and there were 3 different churches meeting under the same roof. The little group who had come from down the street put together a Sunday afternoon "unity service" and invited all 3 groups to come and worship together that afternoon. The leaderships of each group were invited to stand up during the service and share their hearts with the combined crowd. As will happen, the 3 groups filed into the sanctuary and clustered in 3 different sections of the room.

Jason was chosen to speak on behalf of the group he had come with and from. He looked at the section his group was sitting in and said: "God doesn't care that you're (and named the denomination they had come from)... Then he looked at the section with the people I had served with all those years and said: "God doesn't care that you're (and named the denomination we had come from).... Then he looked down at me and the folks from Serenity Church and said: "And God doesn't care that you're—Serenitarian!"

The whole room broke out in laughter. The name stuck. Ask any of us what our church affiliation is and we'll smile and tell you that we're grateful "Serenitarians".

A few days later, the leadership of that little group asked to meet with us. They came to my house, sat down at my table, and said: "We'd like to propose marriage. Serenity Church is where our hearts are. What is happening there is what we were trying so hard to do. We just didn't know how. We aren't suggesting a 'church merger' the way they usually happen–where you take part of what you do, and part of what we do, and do a poor job of doing both. We just want to come and be a full part of what God is doing with Serenity Church. We want to be used. We want to serve those folks–in whatever way you need us."

What they have added to our movement I can't begin to describe. While the heart of us is the roomful of broken "baby Christians" that God keeps leading us to...it simply cannot be done without some deeply rooted, mature Christians that you can absolutely count on.

Within days, God had assembled our first official servant group...our team of Deacons. (Acts 6:1-7, 1 Tim. 3:8-13) Our men and women serve equally and side-by-side in this service to us as they did in the early church. (1 Tim. 3:11, Rom. 16:1) Each of them are mature lifelong Christians who are deeply rooted in Christ, who He is, and how He nurtures His people. They're utterly dependable to see that all the "details" are in place to keep a growing, happy, messy family of God's people moving in the same direction.

As I'm writing this, we have served together in that circle for 6 years. We often don't agree. When we don't, we wait until we do, or we simply trust the hearts of those around us. No matter what, we trust each other's hearts and judgment.

They have seen to it that whatever is needed is provided. 6 years later, Kay and I still live in that house. We have lacked for nothing we have needed.

A couple of years later, we saw a clear need for additional servants covering the bases and the details of the "recovery ministry" which is the heart of who we are and what we do. These needed to be people with long, deep, personal recovery and experience in leading others through that journey. The Recovery Leadership Team was formed with members of our Family with many years of deep roots in the 12-step fellowships. They oversee our Overcomers meetings throughout the week, connect our folks to the other recovery fellowships in our area, and are responsible for the experience of Holy Communion at all of our services. I will explain later that we consider the giving and receiving of Communion to be a profoundly "healing" experience. These folks truly serve at the very heart of who we are.

I'm free to completely give myself to all He has called me to do here—because I know for sure that all the details are being covered by people I can absolutely trust. I would not have known how to even ask for all of that.

Sometimes I feel like Kevin Costner out in a corn field: "If you build it—they will come!"

THIRTY-ONE

Over the last few years, people have found us through the most amazing circumstances and from some astounding locations. I'm regularly contacted by people from all over the U.S. and around the world. The conversations usually begin with something like: "I just knew that somebody had to be doing what you're trying to do. I heard about you (found you online, have a friend of a friend who heard about Serenity Church, has attended a Serenity service, etc, etc). Could you explain to me how we can do that here where I live?" There are a couple of immediate responses to that.

First of all, this is a story that simply can't be told in an email/phone call. That's why our leadership believed so strongly that this book is a priority. As you can already tell—this is not a short story!

The next thing I usually tell them is that we have learned several hundred things that for sure DON'T work...and a handful of things that seem to be right and that God has blessed. When something we're doing appears to be blessed, we pursue it feverishly. If it's not, we discard it just as quickly.

We are determined to be a "movement" and not a "monument". A monument is rigid. It's a stone dedicated to what was. A movement by its very definition is a changing, adapting, flexible thing. Jesus referred to that as a "new wineskin". (Luke 5:36-39)

He said that He will only pour His new thing into a receptacle that can stretch to absorb it when stretching is needed.

As we have desperately tried to do a fresh new thing and hear what God is trying to tell us, we've had to change, adapt, flex, and stretch...a lot! In the next section are a handful of things we have learned (often the "hard way") that we know He has blessed...

THIRTY-TWO

DOES CHRIST REALLY NEED MORE SQUARE FOOTAGE IN HIS REAL ESTATE PORTFOLIO?

Shortly after our first year, we all came to the conclusion that it was time for a fresh start and a new location. Some of the folks that I had served with all of those years under that same roof had a hard time understanding why I had felt the need to go serve "those people" and this new thing and no longer shepherd them. I love them fiercely; but what God was so obviously leading me to do–didn't make sense to many of them. It was strained and awkward at best.

They were also trying to find their way and their identity. Our sometimes overwhelming presence in the middle of their home made that hard for them to do. We began the process of finding a new home, with a fresh start for everybody, for our next chapter.

For many weeks, David and I knocked on more doors, made more phone calls, and drove more miles than we could count... looking for an affordable option for a "place of our own". The ones we could afford didn't have the space we needed. The ones that were big enough–we couldn't afford.

Finally, after weeks of frustration, we seemed to have some sort of epiphany one afternoon. As I told David: "Christ owns literally billions of dollars worth of real estate within minutes of where we're standing. Most of it is locked and dark on Saturday nights. Is adding more square footage to His real estate holdings really how He wants us to invest our very limited resources?"

Through many years of deep involvement in the "Walk To Emmaus" movement, I had a long, deep relationship with a very large church of a mainline denomination in another suburb nearby. I approached them about the possibility of renting space to us on Saturday nights. They welcomed us with open arms and showed us profound hospitality. When Christ said: "I was a stranger and you welcomed me"...I'm pretty sure he had them in mind.

At the same time, we needed a place for our Overcomers Fellowship meetings during the week. Another church, from another mainline denomination, in another community nearby, threw their doors open to us. The Wednesday night that we arrived for our first meeting, their Elders met us at the door with platters of homemade brownies. They hugged each of us as we walked though the door and let us know that people from their church had been coming to the room we'd be meeting in—praying for God's blessing on us as we gather in their home.

For the next 4 years, we met on Saturday nights in a breathtakingly beautiful church campus. We were blessed with tens of millions of dollars of facilities put at our disposal by sweet people who take very seriously the gift of hospitality and the faithful stewardship of what God has given them.

Our initial hope was that we could be a blessing and a resource for them, too. They are a mega-church with thousands of members. It's undeniable that many hundreds of those folks are also involved in the recovery community...or needing/seeking that kind of help. They have no specific recovery ministry.

We made several proposals to them to combine our efforts and help them become a center of spiritual recovery in their community. While very encouraging of our ministry–their leadership did not believe the time was right for them to join forces with us. We saw very few of their folks in our services or meetings.

In the Fall of 2011, a church that was born the same Spring we were...right down the street from where we were born...called us with an intriguing offer. After years in rented spaces, hauling and setting up everything they owned every Sunday, they had recently been given an incredible opportunity to purchase a large 2-story medical/professional office complex. The majority of the building had been empty for years. The owner was a godly Christian dentist who "made them an offer they couldn't refuse". They immediately contacted us and invited us to partner with them in this new chapter...also with an offer we couldn't refuse.

These were folks we had always shared a vision and a deep relationship with. They were also laser-beam focused on reaching those that nobody else was reaching or wanted. Every service of Serenity Church had a crew of their folks with us. All of their services had Serenitarians worshipping and serving with them, too. It had been that way from the beginning.

They were going to gut and remodel that building for a worship center, classrooms, and offices. They offered us full use of all of it...and a suite of offices so we could finally unpack and have a place to operate from 24/7/365. Did I mention "an offer we couldn't refuse?!" In early 2012 we joined them and began our next chapter together.

Let me be clear: I'm definitely not opposed to buildings and facilities for God's people to use for His glory. Wonderful Christians have helped make possible what we do by opening their homes to us. The question is: "Does Christ need more square footage"...to do what He has called US to do...in the place He has called US to do it. Often that answer might be a legitimate "yes". For us, it simply doesn't make sense.

We're a movement—not a location. We're not a "neighborhood church". Our mission is to reach a specific culture not a geographic community. Any time we assemble we will have folks from 15-20 different towns and cities covering a huge radius of geography. We gather up to celebrate, encourage each other, bind up wounds...and then spread out to all of those places we come from.

"The Most High does not live in houses made by men." (Acts 7:48, NIV)

THIRTY-THREE

WHAT I HEARD IN THE DESERT...

"One day Jesus was praying in a certain place. When he finished, one of his disciples said to him, 'Lord, teach us to pray, just as John taught his disciples.' He said to them, when you pray, say: 'Father, hallowed be your name, your kingdom come. Give us each day our daily bread. Forgive us our sins, for we also forgive everyone who sins against us. And lead us not into temptation.' Then he said to them, 'Suppose one of you has a friend, and he goes to him at midnight and says, 'Friend, lend me three loaves of bread, because a friend of mine on a journey has come to me, and I have nothing to set before him.' Then the one inside answers, 'Don't bother me. The door is already locked, and my children are with me in bed. I can't get up and give you anything.' I tell you, though he will not get up and give him the bread because he is his friend, yet because of the man's boldness he will get up and give him as much as he needs. So I say to you: Ask and it will be given to you; seek and you will find; knock and the door will be opened to you. For everyone who asks receives; he who seeks finds; and to him who knocks, the door will be opened. Which of you fathers, if your son asks for a fish, will give him a snake instead? Or if he asks for an egg, will give him a scorpion? If you then, though you are evil, know how to give good gifts to your children, how much more will your Father in heaven give the Holy Spirit to those who ask him!" Luke 11:1–13 (NIV)

June 2008. We celebrated our 2nd "Sereniversary" and launched into our 3rd year. God had blessed us in ways we could not have known how to ask for. The people, the place, the resources that we desperately needed had all been provided. His presence with us was not even debatable. He brought new lives to us–every week. We had a breathtaking front row seat to watch dying people start to live–every week. We were developing the hallmarks of true community and were starting to figure out how to "do this thing".

Now what? What's next, Lord? What do you want us to do? Where would you have us to go? Please don't allow us to just settle into a pleasant rhythm of "doing church". Show us how to keep this movement moving. Don't let us become another spiritual monument.

As usual, I was scheduled to make my twice-a-year pilgrimage to the Monastery that month. As I loaded my car and pointed west I had a very specific agenda this trip. I was going into the desert to clearly hear the will of God for us. I was going for some answers.

For me, there is no place on earth more perfect for just that very thing to happen. The enormity of nature there. The breath-taking beauty of that place. The vacuum silence. The noise of life is turned all the way down so I can actually listen. No phone, no electricity, no internet...there's nothing to drown out what He needs me to hear. Add to that the power of the constant prayer of those godly men day and night. The Enemy has a very hard time getting through to interrupt.

Step Eleven says: "We sought through prayer and meditation to improve our conscious contact with God—praying only for knowledge of His will for us and the power to carry that out".

I asked one of the old-timers early in my recovery what that meant. "Prayer" I thought I understood—but what is this "meditation" thing? The answer I got is still my answer today. Prayer is talking to God. Meditation is quietly listening for His answer.

In the prayer-covered silence of that beautiful place I can hear Christ. I can feel His presence. Over the following days, while I asked and listened, I heard some things very clearly...

I heard in the desert...that SOMETHING IS MISSING. Any time I'm asked to describe the movement of Serenity Church I always answer that it is "the great spiritual adventure of my life"— and it is. It's the truest, purest thing I've ever seen God do. With that said, there is so much to be done—and so few of us doing it.

There are many thousands of people in the recovery communities within minutes of us who are frantically seeking God and know nothing about Christ. How can we be used better, stronger, more. What more do You want from us? What do You want from us now?

So, our prayer becomes: "Father, please show us what we're missing. Please give us what we're missing."

He will answer that prayer. Isn't that what He promised? He said: "Ask and it will be given to you; seek and you will find; knock and the door will be opened to you." Luke 11:9 (NIV)

In case we missed it, he immediately came through the back door and said it again: "For everyone who asks receives; he who seeks finds; and to him who knocks, the door will be opened." Luke 11:10 (NIV)

I heard in the desert...THE POWER OF JESUS' NAME. That's right, His actual name has unimaginable spiritual power. Listen to Paul describe that for us:

"Your attitude should be the same as that of Christ Jesus: Who, being in very nature God, did not consider equality with God something to be grasped, but made himself nothing, taking the very nature of a servant, being made in human likeness. And being found in appearance as a man, he humbled himself and became obedient to death— even death on a cross! Therefore God exalted him to the highest place and gave him the name that is above every name, that at the name of Jesus every knee should bow, in heaven and on earth and under the earth, and every tongue confess that Jesus Christ is Lord, to the glory of God the Father." Philippians 2:5-11 (NIV)

We believe that, don't we? Do we? We close every service of Serenity Church, every meeting of our Overcomers Fellowship, almost every recovery meeting I've ever attended, by reverently praying out loud together: "Our Father, who art in Heaven, hallowed be thy NAME." Do we mean that?

I have a spiritual mentor who told me many years ago that when I feel the attack of the Enemy there's a simple, powerful, fool-proof, guaranteed way to force him to back off. Speak out-loud the words: "Jesus is Lord. Jesus is Lord. Jesus is Lord..." Keep throwing that name in the Enemy's face and he will have no choice but to back off and flee. At the speaking of that name every knee should bow "in Heaven and on earth and under the earth".

My friend was right. Countless times through the years, when the Enemy is attacking, the speaking of that Name has made all the difference for me. God reminded me in the desert that there is a Name that is an incredible weapon when His people speak it.

I heard in the desert...that GOD WANTS TO HEAL US–COMPLETELY. Every great revival of His people has always been accompanied by an outpouring of Divine healing. Why should that surprise us? Jesus called Himself a "doctor". He was clear that he came for the sick ones–like us...

"As Jesus went on from there, he saw a man named Matthew sitting at the tax collector's booth. 'Follow me,' he told him, and Matthew got up and followed him. While Jesus was having dinner at Matthew's house, many tax collectors and 'sinners' came and ate with him and his disciples. When the Pharisees saw this, they asked his disciples, 'Why does your teacher eat with tax collectors and 'sinners'?'" On hearing this, Jesus said, 'It is not the healthy who need a doctor, but the sick. But go and learn what this means: 'I desire mercy, not sacrifice.' For I have not come to call the righteous, but sinners." Matthew 9:9-13 (NIV)

For true, complete healing to happen we're going to have to let Him heal us on several levels. He's going to have to heal our MINDS.

"Therefore, I urge you, brothers, in view of God's mercy, to offer your bodies as living sacrifices, holy and pleasing to God— this is your spiritual act of worship. Do not conform any longer to the pattern of this world, but be transformed by the renewing of your mind. Then you will be able to test and approve what God's will is—his good, pleasing and perfect will." Romans 12:1-2 (NIV)

He can't repair any part of us until He's been allowed to transform and renew our minds.

He's going to have to heal our HEARTS. When Scripture refers to our "hearts", it's generally not referring to the organ that pumps blood. Our hearts are the eternal part of us–the place in us where the Spirit lives. Jesus said: "Blessed are the pure in heart–for they shall see God." I want to see God. That means I'm going to have to allow Him to heal my heart.

He's going to have to heal our BODIES. For most of us that's the toughest of all. My mind and my heart honestly want to be healed and whole. My body is on a completely separate track pulling a completely different direction. Paul said that it's nothing short of a "war" going on inside of us that no one but Christ can win and heal for us...

"I know that nothing good lives in me, that is, in my sinful nature. For I have the desire to do what is good, but I cannot carry it out. For what I do is not the good I want to do; no, the evil I do not want to do—this I keep on doing. Now if I do what I do not want to do, it is no longer I who do it, but it is sin living in me that does it. So I find this law at work: When I want to do good, evil is right there with me. For in my inner being I delight in God's law; but I see another law at work in the members of my body, waging war against the law of my mind and making me a prisoner of the law of sin at work within my members. What a wretched man I am! Who will rescue me from this body of death? Thanks be to God—through Jesus Christ our Lord!" Romans 7:18-25 (NIV)

I heard in the desert...that GOD HONORS PERSISTENT PRAYER. That's what He was trying to teach us in the verses we looked at in Luke 11. He tells the story of a man who is asking his neighbor for help. The neighbor doesn't want to be bothered– but the man keeps asking. Finally, because of his "boldness"...

other translations say "persistence", my favorite is "because of his shameless audacity"....the neighbor gave him what he was asking for.

His point? "How much more will your Father in heaven give the Holy Spirit to those who ask him!" (Luke 11:13) That's what He was asking when He told us to "pray continually". (1 Thessalonians 5:17)

God honors bold, persistent, continual prayer. Not because He's amused by making us beg. He just wants to know that we mean it...that we're willing to keep pursuing the thing we're asking Him to do until it happens...that we'll see it all the way through—as long as it takes.

Praying persistently, continually, is not natural for me. I know that it is for some people. I know a lot of those people. I'm honestly jealous of that ability. My mind wanders. That kind of concentration and focus is hard for me to consistently summon up.

I'd watch the Brothers in the desert who pray full-time. They would hold beads in their hands to help them focus and keep moving in their persistent prayers. I had heard this practice ridiculed my whole life...something about "vain repetitions". Suddenly this made real sense. I had nothing to lose by trying.

I went to the little gift shop they maintain to help support themselves by selling things they make. I bought a set of the beads like the ones that seemed to be helping them focus and keep praying. I went back to my little room in the guesthouse, held them in my hands, and focused on what I had heard over the last several days. Moving through the beads one by one was incredibly helpful in helping me stay focused and persistent.

At the end of the week, as I drove that long drive home, I knew that God had opened my eyes to a fresh way to approach him that would bless my sweet family at Serenity Church and help us keep moving.

The day after I got home I went down to an area of Dallas that is lined for blocks with Asian wholesalers. I went from dealer to dealer until I found what I was looking for...inexpensive bracelets of small polished stones strung on a stretchy cord...with one large stone in the middle where the cord is connected. I emptied my pockets and bought a large bag full of those bracelets.

The following Saturday night, I stood up in front of the Serenitarians and shared with them all that I have just shared with you–that I heard in the holy silence during that week in the desert. I told them that I was committing to God to pray relentlessly for the things He had made so clear He wanted me to be praying. I was making that commitment to God and to them for 40 straight days. If any of them felt called to join me, I'd love their company during this adventure.

Walking over to the communion table I poured out that large pile of those beaded bracelets. "This is how I'm going to be praying for God's blessing of the next chapter of His movement through Serenity Church", I told them, "if any of you would like to join me feel free to pick up a bracelet for yourself before you leave tonight."

...Before starting, sit quietly and make sure that the Enemy is not around to distract you. Simply say out loud: Jesus is Lord, Jesus is Lord, Jesus is Lord...until you feel him back away. He will. He has no choice.

...Holding the large bead, pray: "God, grant me the serenity to accept the things I cannot change, courage to change the things I can, and the wisdom to know the difference."

...Holding the small bead next to it, pray: "Father, please show us what we're missing. Please give us what we're missing. Please heal our minds, and hearts, and bodies–through Christ."

...Move to the next bead and pray that prayer again, the next bead and pray it again—boldly, relentlessly, persistently—all the way around the circle until you have returned to the large bead.

...Pause there and finish like you started: "God, grant me the serenity to accept the things I cannot change, courage to change the things I can, and wisdom to know the difference."

The response was overwhelming. Over 100 bracelets were gone in moments. I went back and got 100 more. Those 40 days were miraculous, life-changing, occasionally even breathtaking. We continued to move–and have never been the same. We've established a rhythm of sharing that experience together every other summer for 40 days. As I type these words, I've just purchased a large load of beaded bracelets. We start the adventure together again next week.

God keeps showing us what we're missing. He constantly gives us what we're missing. Every day He continues to heal our minds, our hearts, and our bodies–through Christ. As long as we persistently ask–He will relentlessly give. The Enemy can't stop a movement like that.

THIRTY-FOUR

WE'RE NOT FOR EVERYBODY

Thursday night has, for a lot of years, been my "meeting night". It's really important that, at least once a week, I sit in a recovery circle where I'm nobody's sponsor, nobody's pastor, nobody's anything. I'm just another one of the anonymous recovering folks in the room.

Periodically, I like to wander into a fresh place where I don't know a soul and just listen to the experience, strength, and hope of total strangers who are winning their battle "one day at a time". Since there are hundreds of recovery groups within minutes of my house, it's not hard to find a new place to be.

One Thursday night, I'd dropped in on a large group in Dallas that I have rarely attended. It was an early evening meeting so I decided to see if there was another one in the area starting soon and make it a double-header. I tracked down another group a few minutes away and got there just in time.

It was a great meeting. On Thursdays they traditionally have a "speaker meeting". One of their folks with a lot of long-time recovery will take all the Thursday nights in a month...and through those meetings will share their story and their journey through the Steps.

This was the first Thursday of the month, so I was there for the first of 4 meetings where this speaker would be sharing his story. It was astounding. I'm going to risk a cliché here and say that for the next hour I was literally "on the edge of my seat". He's a surgeon at a large Dallas hospital with nearly 20 years of recovery. He had been to the gates of Hell and back. I made the decision before he finished talking that night that I'd be back for the next 3 Thursdays to hear the rest of his story.

The group met on one end of a strip center on the edge of a pretty tough neighborhood. I inevitably had to park toward the other end which was anchored by a little store-front church. Each week as I came and went, I'd notice the sign lettered on the plate glass window on the front of the church. It had the church's name, phone number, web address...and then in bold italics it said: "The love of God is for everyone..."

Something about that really struck me. It just sounded so "Serenitarian". Who were these people? Finally, after 2-3 weeks of this, when I got home I looked up their website and started clicking around.

When I clicked over to the "Pastor" page I paused. His name sounded so familiar. There was a link to email him so I shot him a quick email that just said: "Do I know you?" Within minutes Allen replied: "YES you know me!"

He went on to remind me that when I was pastoring the large church where I hit bottom and found recovery–he was pastoring a neighboring church of the same denomination. A couple of years later, he had come to see me about starting a recovery ministry at their church and had me in to speak to his church.

A lot of water had gone under the bridge in the 20 years since then. He had gone on to a very "successful" ministry at a flagship church in California. An unravelling marriage had finally blown apart, his ex-wife had moved out-of-state with their 4 sons. Their church no longer had a place for him.

In complete despair he had spiraled deep into a pit of prescription painkillers trying to make the pain go away. Finally, after inpatient treatment and recovery he had moved to be near his sons and help finish raising them. His boys were now grown, starting families of their own, and making their way in the world.

Through all of that he had never lost the "call" to preach and pastor. He knew that's what God intended for him to do. Was it even possible now? Would anybody want what he had to offer? A very dear mutual friend of ours had begun to search and found this little church in Dallas that was looking for a pastor. They had invited him to move to Dallas as their pastor, and God had relaunched his ministry.

It was a complicated, challenging ministry by any definition. They were situated in a place to minister two directions to two groups who were profoundly disenfranchised by most evangelical churches. To the south, they were reaching out with the love of Christ to one of the largest gay neighborhoods in America. To the north, they were trying to take that same love and compassion to a desperately poor neighborhood overrun with homeless people.

"Challenging" was actually an understatement. They would desperately try to take a positive step forward and inevitably would be knocked two steps back.

In the months that followed, Allen and I formed a deep, supportive friendship. Our churches began to connect, encourage, and support each other. Within a year or so, though, it became clear that their little church was finally running out of steam.

Their folks were tired, discouraged, and simply didn't have the resources to do what they were trying to do. They were making the decision to disband.

After a lot of prayer, I brought a suggestion to our leadership that was immediately, enthusiastically embraced. We sat down with their leadership and offered an alternative.

Rather than "disband" and drift apart...what about taking a "breather" while they refocused, got back on their feet, and relaunched? They had invested years in relationships with each other. Stay together. Come meet with us for the next year or so. We would earmark all of their tithes to continue to support Allen. He could continue to minister to them...and to us. When they had caught their breath and decided they were ready, we would help them relaunch their church.

At first, that plan was enthusiastically embraced by them. As we got closer to making it happen, though, they decided that their church had simply run its course. They would just come join us and share our fellowship. We promised that their tithes would still all be set apart to support Allen and his ministry.

For the next few months, it seemed like a grand experiment that just might work. They were with us on Saturday nights... and every Tuesday night they met at Allen's house for a meal and a Bible study.

No matter how hard we reached out to them and tried to weave them into our Family, we began to notice they were drifting away and we saw less and less of them. Within 6 months Allen was the only one left in our regular fellowship.

At first, I was really confused...and a little hurt. What had we done, or not done, that kept them from absorbing into our fellowship? It was Allen who helped me put the pieces in place. Here's the point:

WE'RE NOT FOR EVERYBODY.

Serenity Church is a very unique fellowship, given a very specific mission, to speak Christ to a very specific culture, in the language they speak and understand.

Those sweet folks didn't lose their faith or leave Christ. Just the opposite–Christ is continuing to use them, nurture them, and speak to them in a wide variety of settings and venues where He needs them to be. They simply don't identify with where we come from...and speak truth the way we speak it...in the language that we understand.

Allen continued to feed them physically and spiritually in his home every week. They continued to encourage and support Serenity Church. All of that made possible by some wonderful Christians who just happen to see the world through the lens of a different culture that expresses itself in a different way.

I used to consider multiple gatherings in a community, speaking Christ in a variety of ways, to be a great failure. Nothing could be further from the truth. The truth for us today: WE'RE NOT FOR EVERYBODY.

There's a chapter ahead that speaks of the singleness of our mission. We'll get back to that. God has a wonderful variety of fellowships and spokespeople to bring one message to many people in the way that they can hear it.

Amen to that!

THIRTY-FIVE

NEVER ALONE AGAIN

There were just 4 of us in the first meetings of our Overcomers Fellowship nearly 25 years ago. I was less than 2 years into my recovery. We had just moved to the little country town where we would raise our kids. The original handful of us met in our living room and began to put the pieces together that are still the heart of our Overcomers meetings today...and would eventually birth Serenity Church.

We tracked down the mint that produces the coins and medallions for thousands of recovery groups and ordered their catalog. The months/anniversary medallions were obvious choices for our first order. We decided that we wanted something special, though, to welcome anyone that God led to us for the first time.

A large section of the catalog was devoted to "affirmation medallions". These didn't specifically mark milestones of recovery. They were simply engraved with slogans and principles of recovery on one side and the Serenity Prayer on the back of most of them. We began the tradition then, that continues to this day, of ordering a different affirmation medallion each month. Everybody who attends our meetings during that month is given one and our meetings concentrate on that principle.

As we were going through the catalog, Calvin spotted one that said it all to him. "That's it", he said, "that's our story!" He pointed to one that simply said: "NEVER ALONE AGAIN"

He went on to explain to us that this was the thing we all have in common. There are as many reasons for sitting in that circle as there are people in the room. No matter what it was that hurt us–when we were in the bottom of that pit we truly felt that we were alone there. Now we have each other. From now on we're NEVER ALONE AGAIN.

We ordered those coins and have given one to everybody who walks in and sits in those circles with us. Over the decades since, thousands of people have been given a tangible reminder that they have the choice to never be in that dark place by themselves again.

Calvin lived that truth as purely as anybody I've shared recovery with. Week after week, and then year after year, there was one thing you knew for sure: when you walked through the door looking for those answers Calvin would be there with a bear hug and a welcome. He'd make sure you weren't alone.

Years later, we left there to go serve another church and began planting those seeds of recovery all over again. Several years after we moved, I got a phone call from Calvin's family. He had been on his way to work that morning and an 18-wheeler had crashed into the side of his truck as he tried to cross a busy highway by his auto mechanic shop. He had died instantly. They wanted to know if I'd come back and help them bury Calvin.

The next night I arrived at the funeral home. I walked up to the casket that held Calvin's body...all dressed up in a suit and tie. I reached in my pocket and took out a very familiar silver medallion and slipped it in his pocket. I thanked God for all the Calvins in my life who make sure that I'm never alone again.

There are few things more basic in human beings than for the "me" to become "we"...the "I" to become "us". It's a deep, desperate, primal need. That's why churches tend to form around groups of people who think alike, understand alike, speak alike, hear alike.

The problem with most of us at the bottom of our brokeness is that we feel we are terminally unique. My pain is special to me. You can't possibly understand. That's why the two most healing words that one human being can speak to another are: "I know..." I've been where you are. I've hurt like you hurt.

I've said countless times over the last 25 years that I can never fully trust anybody who has never been significantly broken. Oh, I'll love you. I'll be your friend. But when I find myself face down in the dirt again–and I will...when I need to reach up and grab a hand to pull me up again–and I will...you are not the one I'm going to be looking for. I'm going to reach for the people in my life who can look me right in the eye and say: "I know...I've been right where you are...and this is the way out of that hole you're in."

A key way to identify people like us is the way that we express ourselves. Catholics have a way of expressing their faith that makes them "us" with other Catholics. So do Methodists, Baptists, Boy Scouts, Rotarians and Republicans. When you speak my language to me, I know that the two of us are "we".

The recovery community probably senses that, and needs that, as desperately as any other culture. Before I can hear you, I need for you to speak it in the language that tells me you are "us". When Serenity Church assembles we never forget that.

A couple of years ago, Kay and I attended a service of a church that is deeply rooted in liturgy. She and I don't come from a liturgical tradition. On the way home I commented on how beautiful the service was. I said: "but, you know, I don't think I would do well in a setting that came back to repeating the same liturgy to each other week-after-week and year-after-year." She instantly broke out in a belly laugh over that. She said: "John, you do understand, don't you, that Serenity Church is probably the most liturgical church in town!"

Whoops! Once again she was absolutely right. When the AA drunk, the NA junkie, etc, etc, walk through that door to see if "we" are actually "them"—it's critical that they hear the language spoken by us that they heard in the meeting at their home group the night before.

Our services always open with with the Serenity Prayer prayed out loud in unison. Early in the service one of us will come to the front and lead us in speaking together the 12-steps. In my sermons I will quote the Apostle Paul one moment and Biblically based spiritual truth from the AA Big Book the next. We close all our services by standing for a reading of the 12 Promises from the Big Book and close by speaking together the Lord's Prayer. We speak the language they heard in their meetings through the week so they know that we are who they are.

Remember that I had committed to God that I would be a part of this nearly 20 years before Serenity Church was finally born. In the early '90s, I heard that the Saddleback Church in California was in the process of beginning a new movement to bring recovery to the church that they were calling "Celebrate Recovery". I was thrilled! I have a deep and profound respect for Rick Warren. If he was part of this, if it was happening under his leadership, I was extremely confident it was going to be a very good thing. Maybe we wouldn't have to "invent the wheel" after all. If they were already doing this thing I had committed to God to do...maybe I could just jump on their train with them!

I took the very first opportunity to go to Saddleback for a week of training in what this new thing is and how it works. I left as impressed as I expected to be—but I was still not off the hook. They had identified, and were addressing powerfully, a desperately needed empty place in the recovery world. They were translating the power of the recovery community into the language of the church. People in the church who might not ever walk into an AA hall could access that same power in the language of the people in the pew.

People ask me constantly: what is the difference between Serenity Church/Overcomers Fellowship and Celebrate Recovery? I believe we are mirrored images of each other...two halves of a whole. Celebrate Recovery does an astounding job of translating the principles of the recovery community into the language of the church. Serenity/Overcomers translates the message of Christ and the church and speaks it in the language of the recovery community. We each need to hear the message in our own language.

What we do is reproducible wherever our language is spoken. In 2011, God gave birth to our first baby Serenity Church in Longview, Texas. In 2012, Serenity Church was launched in Tyler, Texas, and in a desperately poor, drug infested, neighborhood in South Dallas. It's our prayer and belief that this movement will continue to move in countless places our message is desperately needed. God, please take our little bit and multiply it. Make us a movement and not a monument.

THIRTY-SIX

HOLY MOMENTS

The most wonderful discovery in this new way of life are the times when we can reach out and touch Christ. This journey has stops all along the way where His presence is palpable. Scripture says to reach for Him with "shameless audacity". There are times in this walk when his reaching back is so shamelessly audacious that it literally takes your breath away. There are times when He allows us to reach out and touch Him—and in some very real way He touches us back.

There have been countless of those moments in my life—before and after my recovery. He didn't just show up, frantically trying to touch me, after I found the 12-Steps. He has always, relentlessly, loudly tried to show Himself to me in some very real, touchable way.

The night I sat on the back steps of that treatment center while God reminded me that He uses His people best after they have been completely broken and allowed Him to rebuild them. That was a Holy Moment.

Sitting on the side of a concrete grill at a roadside picnic area praying and burning the hurts of my lifetime. That was a Holy Moment.

Sitting in a tiny holding cell of a penitentiary listening, absorbing the pain, and offering grace to sobbing men as they let go of the wounds that are literally killing them. That's a Holy Moment.

Standing up every Saturday night and looking across a roomful of people–many of whom might very well might be dead if God hadn't led them there. Those are always Holy Moments.

I mentioned that our family spent significant time living in the deepest, remotest jungles of Nigeria when I was a kid. That's not an exaggeration. The "witch doctor" was the primary religious figure in most of the villages around us. We went to sleep every night to the pounding of drums, screaming, and chanting while our neighbors gathered to worship a giant old cottonwood tree that was the home of the local "god". Cannibalism was regularly and openly practiced.

We lived in a concrete block house with a tin roof, no electricity, phone or running water. This was an unimaginably extravagant lifestyle to our neighbors who all lived in mud houses with thatch roofs.

We lived in constant danger. Locals who bitterly opposed our presence there, others who could sell our corpses to a nearby meat market at a premium, others who practiced the ancient occult religions of that area who considered us a threat to their way of life. There were people on all sides who would prefer for us to be dead.

So that we could sleep safely at night, our concrete block house had bars installed in all the windows, a thick slab of wood for doors, and we hired a local "night watchman" who stood guard with a machete and a shotgun while we slept.

One night, just after dark, a man from the village came to our door desperate to get his wife to the hospital. We had the only car for many miles in any direction. It was an old Volkswagen Beetle that could straddle the paths through the jungle and eventually get us to the nearest actual road. By car, the nearest hospital was nearly 2 hours away. Without a car, that woman was likely to die that night.

My Dad hurriedly put them in our car, saw that his family was safely locked in for the night, and left our safety in the hands of our night watchman.

Not long after they left, our night watchman got seriously drunk on some local palm wine. The drunker he got, the more convinced he became that outsiders really had no business living in his village. He began to pound on our door screaming that he had decided that we needed to die. He was going to get in that house and chop us all to pieces.

My mom was locked into that house alone with her 7 year old son and 4 year old daughter. Most people would be justifiably hysterical with panic at a moment like that. Most people are not my Mom.

She pulled out our Egermeier's Bible Story Book, sat down on the couch with me on one side of her and my sister on the other, and began to read to us. For hours. While a drunk man with a shotgun and a machete pounded at our door screaming his promise to kill us all.

Much later that night my Dad returned home to that scene: a drunk man on our front porch, with a machete and a shotgun, screaming threats to kill us. Absolutely furious, my Dad charged toward him. Looking for any sort of weapon to arm himself with, all he could immediately lay his hands on was the night watchman's kerosene lantern. He grabbed it, began swinging it in the air, and chased a fully armed man deep into the jungle...in the dark...armed with nothing but a kerosene lantern!

Over 50 years later, we celebrated my Mom's 80th birthday last year. I desperately wanted to find the perfect gift. I wanted to give her some thing that summed up to me who she is. I found it after some serious searching online: a 1950s edition of Egermeier's Bible Story Book. Exactly like the one she read to us that night while she faced down death and protected her children...in a truly Holy Moment.

That was a holy thing in my hands as I gave it to her that day. It physically represents a holy moment. She was thrilled by it and did exactly what I would expect her to do. After asking my permission, she gave it to my daughter to read to my grandchildren.

****

My Senior year in high school I worked after school as a sacker at a neighborhood Piggly Wiggly grocery store. One night after work, I got home and called my girlfriend. She asked if I'd eaten dinner yet. I told her I hadn't had time. She said: "We had steaks tonight. There's one left and the grill's still hot. Why don't you come over, and we'll have it ready by the time you get here."

On my way out the door, my Mom told me to be sure and wear my glasses. I usually only wore them to drive and kept them under the driver's seat. About halfway there, I remembered that I had promised to wear them and reached under the seat to get them.

I took my eyes off the road for that quick moment. As I did, I veered to the right and head-on into a telephone pole. The impact was so quick, and so complete that my head came down face first and broke off the steering wheel and the gear shift lever on the steering column of my 1965 Plymouth Fury. My head recoiled back, went through the windshield, and then pulled back through the shattered glass.

There was very little left of what had been my face. My left ear was pulled loose and dangling upside down. A section of my skull was exposed through a gash in my forehead. My nose had been obliterated. My upper lip was ripped loose and dangling down toward my chin. My left eyebrow was hanging down over my eye.

Miraculously, I was still conscious. In shock—but conscious. I was completely blinded because both eyes were swollen shut. I had enough awareness to know I needed to get to help. Miracle #2, I remembered where I was.

The part of town I was driving through included the large estates of most of the wealthiest families in the city. I was about a half a block from the long circular driveway that lead to one of those estates. I started feeling my way along the curb trying to find that driveway. As I stumbled down the street, I began to pat myself trying to take some kind of blind inventory of what kind of shape I was in. Everything I touched was soaked with blood.

My first thought? I can't go to those people's house looking like this. Did I mention I was in shock?! I felt my way back to my car, got in, and turned the key. Completely blind, I was going to drive myself somewhere. Nothing happened. Of course, it's not in "Park". I groped around trying to find the gear shift lever. It was gone. I couldn't find the steering wheel. I was going to have to feel my way to those people's house before I bled to death.

The next part is pretty foggy, but (Miracle #3) I made my way to that driveway, past their horse stables and tennis courts, and to their front door. It's a grand, colonial, columned mansion with the big double doors at the main entrance. Over the doors was a little semi-circular balcony accessed by French doors on the 2nd floor. Blinded, I couldn't find the door bell. With my lip ripped loose from my face, I couldn't make words. All I could do was stand on their porch, scream, and pray that somebody would hear me before I bled to death.

Miracle #4, behind the French doors upstairs right above me was the study of the man who lived there. He was on the phone, with the doors closed, with music playing...and heard me screaming. He came out on the balcony, saw me below, and screamed downstairs to his wife to let me in. I can only imagine what a horror that must have been to encounter on their porch. They had me lie down on the floor, called for an ambulance, found out my name from my driver's license in my wallet, and called my folks. They got there just in time to follow the ambulance to the hospital.

The first thing they did was to call our family doctor. He was rushing through the hospital to the ER and "coincidentally" literally bumped into one of the most gifted plastic surgeons in the state. He wasn't there as a doctor that night. He was there to visit his mother who was recovering from surgery that day. Our doctor grabbed him by the arm and rushed with him to the ER to see the boy who no longer had a face.

Before they wheeled me into surgery, the surgeon came out and asked my folks if they had a picture of me. There was very little left to give him clues what I was supposed to look like.

With a school picture from my Mom's wallet he began the long process of building a face where one used to be.

You're probably asking, "where's the Holy Moment in all of that mess?!" It's a simple answer: who I am profoundly changed that night. As I lay in that hospital bed through a long, tough recovery, it dawned on me that this was simply not possible. This could not happen. The human skull is not designed to withstand an impact violent enough to shatter the steering wheel and break the gear shift lever off the column of a '65 Plymouth. If, against all odds, someone survived that...they most definitely would not still have the ability to walk a serious distance completely blinded and find help in time not to die. I had been saved. Clearly, indisputably, miraculously saved.

I had never really liked me. I had always felt profoundly useless. Everything I had tried to succeed at, I had failed miserably. In spite of desperately trying, I am not athletic. I'm not musical. I'm not mechanical. I'm not artistic. I'm not a gifted scholar. I'm not any of the things that a 17 year-old wants to be to feel worthy.

With all of that, God had obviously gone to astounding lengths to save me for something. It seemed inconceivable to me that I had survived all of that for no purpose. He had something really significant for me to do–and had saved me to do it. Who I understood myself to be was never the same after that night.

I had a LONG way to go to finally let down my walls and accept the "miraculous", but an unshakable seed was planted that night that made that acceptance possible for me years later. How could I permanently deny the existence of miracles–when I so clearly AM ONE?!

Less than a year later, I was finishing up my first semester of my freshman year of college. I was scheduled during Christmas break to have the last surgery to put my face back together. There was one more major scar that needed to be addressed. As the time got close I asked my folks to cancel the surgery. I was going to keep that scar.

I've never regretted that decision. All I have to do is look in the mirror. From right under my nose across to my cheek, there's a permanent reminder that I'm a living, breathing miracle. My life was spared on purpose. I have refused to believe that God went to all of that effort for nothing. He has something significant to Him for me to do.

****

In 1998, my Dad's health began to fail. He was having increasing difficulty breathing. For a variety of reasons, including the long term effects of the drugs that treated his severe rheumatoid arthritis, the lining of his lungs had started to harden. There really wasn't much the doctors could do. We watched him slow down and decline alarmingly quickly.

In early March of 1999, we got a call from my Mom as we walked in the door from Sunday services. When my Dad woke up that morning, he was blue and couldn't breathe. She had rushed him to the hospital. Kay and I jumped in the car and broke every traffic law getting there in record time.

By the time we got there, he was having oxygen pumped into his lungs, had his color back, was sitting up in bed, and "holding court" entertaining and amusing everybody around him.

After we had visited for a few minutes, he turned to my Mom and said: "I was visiting with a couple of the nurses on the hall here and they both have small children. I just got a case of Bibles for Parents in the mail the other day. Would you mind going to the house and pick up a couple of those. I'd like for them to both have one." My Mom left to go get the Bibles.

He turned to Kay and said: "You know what I'd love more than anything right now? A large chocolate milk shake! Could I talk you into bringing me one?" Kay left to get a milk shake.

When it was just the two of us left, he turned to me and said: "We've talked about this before. You know what I want—but let's go over it one more time. I don't want a funeral. I want a party. A true celebration. There's nothing to grieve here. It's all good! I'd like to be cremated. Scatter some of my ashes on the family plot where my parents and grandparents are buried...and any other place where you think I ought to be. I'd like a stone put down there beside them. Engrave on it my name, my dates, and then have them engrave for generations to see: 'I HAD A BALL!'... because I have! Make sure there's an exclamation point. I've had more fun in 71 years than most men would get in several life-times!"

He had several other instructions and reminders—and just as he finished my Mom showed up with the Bibles and Kay walked in with a huge milk shake. That night he lost consciousness and never regained it. Later that week God took him Home.

We did everything he asked just as he requested. We had a huge celebration for him. He would have loved it! When my Mom, my sister, and I were making the arrangements at the funeral home, I noticed shelves on the wall with a variety of urns. I picked a small one that could be sealed when it had been filled. I asked the funeral director to fill and seal it for me when the ashes arrived from the crematory—and he did.

That little urn has been to some wonderful places. It sits in my study, and there have been countless times that I have just reached over and picked it up and felt his presence at a time I needed to feel him. It sat right beside me when I performed the weddings for both of his grandchildren. It was at the front by the pulpit the night Serenity Church was born. He would love Serenity Church! So often, I've wished he could have lived to know the Serenitarians and to stand up on a Saturday night and share his faith with them. The truth? He does just that every week—through those of us he poured himself into.

So, what do an antique children's Bible story book, a scar on my face, and an urn of ashes have to do with God, healing, and holiness?!

God has always known that we human beings respond through our senses. We need to touch, taste, hear, smell, and see things in order for them to truly be "real" to us. Sometimes, we just can't get there any other way. We are spiritual beings in a physical world. That's not bad or wrong. He made us that way. All through history He has made allowances for that.

Holding that book in my hands, and presenting it as a gift to the woman who has always nurtured me, made a very Holy Moment—from very long ago—alive and real right now.

When I look in the mirror and I see the years etched on my face—that scar presents to me all over again that I am a walking, breathing, miracle preserved by God for a purpose He had in mind for me since before I was born. He didn't allow a teenager's careless driving to change His purpose for me.

When I have that little urn in my hand, when it sits beside me in the Holy Moments of my life, my Dad is present with me in a way that a mere memory can't accomplish. Is my Dad in that little jar? Of course not! He's not even dead. He's more alive right now than we can even imagine. Still, to hold that in my hand makes him more real to me in the way that we humans need and understand.

God understands that about us. Through the ages, He has given His people physical moments where He touches us and allows us to touch Him back.

Often, these moments are referred to as "Sacraments" or Sacred Moments. They vary some from one faith tradition to another. Depending on your background, they may include a wide variety of Holy Moments where God touches us.

But there are two of these Sacred Moments that are embraced and practiced by Christians of many traditions. They are the holiest moments we will experience in this life. They are physical moments where God touches us—and allows us to touch Him back. They are particularly powerful and precious to Serenity Church because we believe He designed both of these as supernatural healing times for broken people like us.

THIRTY-SEVEN

BURYING THE OLD YOU

The first of these sacred moments is BAPTISM. We read about the baptism of John the Baptizer. We hear the story of Jesus modeling the power of it by asking His cousin John to baptize Him, too. But how did that get brought to us?

To put the pieces of that story together, we really have to go back to an especially frustrating time in Jesus' ministry...

Matthew 16:13-20 (NIV)....When Jesus came to the region of Caesarea Philippi, he asked his disciples, "Who do people say the Son of Man is?" They replied, "Some say John the Baptist; others say Elijah; and still others, Jeremiah or one of the prophets." "But what about you?" he asked. "Who do you say I am?" Simon Peter answered, "You are the Christ, the Son of the living God." Jesus replied, "Blessed are you, Simon son of Jonah, for this was not revealed to you by man, but by my Father in heaven. And I tell you that you are Peter, and on this rock I will build my church, and the gates of Hades will not overcome it. I will give you the keys of the kingdom of heaven; whatever you bind on earth will be bound in heaven, and whatever you loose on earth will be loosed in heaven."

Bless his heart, Jesus just couldn't catch a break with His preaching! He had gone from town to town preaching His heart out to people who had supposedly been anxiously watching for His arrival for centuries. He had fed them, healed them, raised the dead, and forgiven the broken. He had explained simply and clearly who He was, why He was here, what He had come to do. After all of that—nobody seemed to get it!

Finally, deeply frustrated, He gathered together His twelve closest friends...those who had witnessed all of that and knew Him best. He asked them a simple question: "Who do people think I am?"

They came up with a variety of answers that all had one thing in common. They were all dead! Basically, they were saying, "Folks are convinced you're some kind of ghost or something."

Jesus looked at the ones who knew Him best and tried again: "How about you? Who do you think I am?" Who do you think might leap in first here?

I do love Peter. Mostly, because he is so much like...me. He was constantly shooting his mouth off at some very wrong times. Over and over Jesus would have to get in his face and tell him to shut up! That didn't change on this day, either. Look just 4 verses later and Peter is already back to inappropriately spouting off—and Jesus is back in his face again telling him to get back and hush: "Get behind me, Satan! You are a stumbling block to me..." (16:23) Sometimes you're just the Devil, Peter. Don't make me crawl over you to get where I'm going...

This time, though, Peter's instantly shooting his mouth off without thinking paid off. I can practically hear him shout the answer: "You are the Christ, the Son of the living God."

Can't you almost feel Jesus' relief? Somebody gets it. Somebody understands me, who I am, why I'm here. He turns to him and said: "Blessed are you, Simon son of Jonah, for this was not revealed to you by man, but by my Father in heaven..."

"Peter" was not actually his name. His name was Simon. Since there were a lot of Simons in that part of the world at that time, he would also identify himself by who his dad was. His name was "Simon son of Jonah". Peter was a nickname given to him by Jesus. This is when that happened.

Jesus had a great sense of humor. He was really funny. He especially loved a good pun. Unfortunately, puns usually don't travel well from one language to another so we generally completely miss them. This moment is a perfect example. Basically, the conversation went like this...

From now on, Simon, I'm going to start calling you Peter ("Petros"–which means a little rock, a pebble)... But on this "Petra" (a large rock, a boulder) I will build my church..You may just be a pebble but you just spoke a boulder of truth...On this giant truth you just spoke: that I am, in fact, "the Christ"–I'm going to build my church. Not even death (the gates of Hades) will stop that from happening. Because you were the one who "gets it", when it comes time to open my Kingdom to the whole world I'm going to let you turn the key and open that door to everybody for all time.

Time passed. Jesus kept preaching. People kept misunderstanding who He was and what He was here to do. Our Pebble is still getting in trouble with his Big Rock Complex–blowing, blustering, and shooting his mouth off at the wrong times.

Jesus died, came back out of His grave, finished His physical ministry here, and told His inner circle that He was going back where He came from to get a place ready for all of us. It's time now to throw open the doors and finally invite the whole world into his Kingdom. He told them to go wait in Jerusalem for the next chapter of the story. What they had waited for so long was finally coming.

Not long after this, He rose in a cloud to go get ready for us. There was a a huge crowd assembling in Jerusalem for a major Jewish holiday in Acts 2. Fifty days after Passover, Jews from all over the world converged on Jerusalem to gather at the Great Temple and celebrate the Feast of Pentecost.

Jesus' inner circle of close friends had gathered in the Temple to celebrate with them. Suddenly, several astounding things started happening all at once. First, a deafening roaring noise like a whirlwind overwhelmed all the usual crowd noises in the Temple. Right on the heels of that, fire came down and settled on the heads of the twelve Apostles...and they suddenly began to preach. This was no ordinary preaching, though. Jews from all over the world, who spoke an incredible variety of different languages, all understood what they were saying in their own languages.

To say the least, they had the crowd's attention! Just once in a lifetime of preaching I'd love to have a moment where my sermon is accompanied by a whirlwind, fire shooting up from the top of my head, and a dozen or so languages coming out of my mouth at the same time. That would pretty much assure a preacher's credibility!

In the middle of all of that confusion, we know who we're going to hear from. He had earned this privilege by affirming Christ at the moment He most desperately needed it. The doors of the Kingdom are finally about to be thrown open to the whole world. It's time to use those "keys" Christ had given him. "Then Peter stood up with the Eleven, raised his voice and addressed the crowd..." (Acts 2:14)

He told them that none of this should be a surprise to any of them. The Prophets had been telling the Jews for centuries that this moment was coming, what to look for, and what to expect. He told them about Jesus, who He was, what He had done, what He was doing. Then he dropped a bombshell on them:

"Men of Israel, listen to this: Jesus of Nazareth was a man accredited by God to you by miracles, wonders and signs, which God did among you through him, as you yourselves know. This man was handed over to you by God's set purpose and foreknowledge; and you, with the help of wicked men, put him to death by nailing him to the cross. But God raised him from the dead, freeing him from the agony of death, because it was impossible for death to keep its hold on him." (2:22-24, NIV)

It's hard to imagine the horror that rolled through the crowd at that moment. Some of these people listening to Peter that morning had undoubtedly been in that mob demanding that Christ be killed. They would have been at Pilate's palace screaming: "Crucify him! Crucify him!" Now, there can't be any question about what they had done and to Whom they had done it. When a man stands up in a whirlwind, with fire on his head, and tells you something in dozens of languages all at once—you really can't deny his authenticity.

"When the people heard this, they were cut to the heart and said to Peter and the other apostles, "Brothers, what shall we do?" (2:37)

No kidding. What possible answer could they expect to hear? What would be sufficient to make up for what they had done. They had tortured to death God's "only begotten Son". What makes up for that? I'm confident what my answer would have been. If you slowly, unspeakably tortured my child to death...

and I got to choose what happened to you in return...I'm confident I'd want you to suffer every bit as much as you caused the one I love to suffer.

It's time for Peter to turn that "key". His answer to their question is THE answer for all time. It will be breathtaking and outrageous...

"Peter replied, 'Repent and be baptized, every one of you, in the name of Jesus Christ for the forgiveness of your sins. And you will receive the gift of the Holy Spirit'." (2:38)

What?! Really?! To atone for murdering Christ, God wants them to do two things—and they'll receive two things in return.

He said: "repent"... That word really means more than just "be sorry". It means "go in a different direction". You were walking that way? Stop—and walk this way instead. Stop going where you were going. Stop doing what you were doing. "Repent".

He said: "be baptized"... Paul will explain to us shortly more of what that means.

If we do those two things, God will give us two things in return...

"Peter replied, "Repent and be baptized, every one of you, in the name of Jesus Christ for the forgiveness of your sins. And you will receive the gift of the Holy Spirit."

Not only will ALL of our sins—past, present, and future—cease to exist...a piece of God will come to live inside of us to help us live the life He created us to live.

Here's the Good News in all of that for us... That very same set of promises applies to us just like it did for them. When

Peter turned those keys and threw open that door, it was for all of humanity for all time. How do we know that? Listen to his very next words:

"The promise is for you and your children and for all who are far off—for all whom the Lord our God will call." (2:39)

Almost immediately, the first Christians were overwhelmed by the Grace of God that could, and would, forgive absolutely anything. It's so complete that it could actually take away the guilt of murdering Jesus.

It didn't take long, though, for people to take that gift in places God never intended for it to go. The reasoning went something like this... If God's Grace can forgive absolutely anything—then let's sin a BUNCH and get more of God's Grace! I'd like to pause and be morally outraged here—but, unfortunately, I have the kind of sick mind that could make sense out of that nonsense if I wanted to badly enough!

Paul finally wrote to the church in Rome and confronted this foolishness head-on...

"What shall we say, then? Shall we go on sinning so that grace may increase? By no means! We died to sin; how can we live in it any longer? Or don't you know that all of us who were baptized into Christ Jesus were baptized into his death? We were therefore buried with him through baptism into death in order that, just as Christ was raised from the dead through the glory of the Father, we too may live a new life. If we have been united with him like this in his death, we will certainly also be united with him in his resurrection. For we know that our old self was crucified with him so that the body of sin might be done away with, that we should no longer be slaves to sin..." (Romans 6:1-6, NIV)

Remember that Peter used two keys to unlock that door for us. When we "repent", we stop walking the direction we were going and start walking the direction Christ is pointing us. If we're walking the way we used to–we're not walking in "repentance".

He follows that up with a powerful description of what happens through the miracle of "baptism". "We were therefore buried with him through baptism into death...If we have been united with him like this in his death, we will certainly also be united with him in his resurrection."

For us, this is the miraculous, supernatural moment where the "old us" is proclaimed dead and officially buried. When we are buried in that water, we leave who we were in that "grave". Christ died, was buried, and came out of His grave never to have to die again. It's the same for us. Who we were dies, is buried, and when we come up out of that grave we are immortal. We never have to die again. We are "united with him in his resurrection".

Sure, unless Christ comes for us soon, our bodies are all going to wear out and stop working. That has nothing to do with "death" for us. We share His resurrection.

THIRTY-EIGHT

THE MEAL THAT HEALS

The second Sacred Moment, where we are allowed to "touch" God and He touches us back, is the sharing of the meal of Holy Communion. There are two ways this Holy Moment touches us with the Grace of God.

First of all, this is the moment that makes me a part of you—and you a part of me. In one of his letters to the church in Corinth, Paul explains a remarkable thing that happens when we share Christ's meal. He said: "Is not the cup of thanksgiving for which we give thanks a participation in the blood of Christ? And is not the bread that we break a participation in the body of Christ?"

But then He took it a full step further: "Because there is one loaf, we, who are many, are one body, for we all partake of the one loaf." (1 Corinthians 10:16-17)

Years ago, this hit me in a whole new way the first time I saw the movie "Places in the Heart". Set during the Depression in the part of Texas where I live, it told the story of a husband and father of three small children who was shot and killed in a tragic accident. The young black man who shot him was drunk at the time. He didn't mean to do it. They were friends. It was an accident. In that part of the world, during that chapter of our history, none of that mattered. He was caught and lynched for it that very same day.

The young widow was left destitute and was about to lose her home in a bank foreclosure. She decided, against all odds, to struggle to keep her home and raise a crop of cotton to keep their family intact.

A drifter came through, an unemployed black man named Moses, who helped her harvest her cotton and save her home. Eventually, though, Moses is run out of town by the Ku Klux Klan. They deeply resented the concept of a smart, capable black man. That process was started by the gin operator who didn't appreciate the shrewd business advice that Moses had given the young widow. Several other lives unfolded in the telling of the story—including a young couple whose marriage had been torn apart by unfaithfulness.

In the closing scene of the film, the congregation is gathered to worship. The preacher has just finished reading 1 Corinthians 13... "Now these three remain: faith, hope, and love, but the greatest of these is love."

Holy Communion is being passed through the congregation. As the people take the bread and cup, you are suddenly aware that this is no ordinary congregation. The camera zooms in.

There's the widow sitting beside Moses who had been run out of town. The widow's dead husband is sitting beside her on the other side. Sitting next to him is the young man who shot him and was killed for it. The banker is there who tried to take away her home—and the cotton gin operator who tried to destroy her. There are members of the Ku Klux Klan sitting beside a pew full of black tenant farmers. The couple whose marriage had been torn apart are there—reconciled to each other.

Without a word being said, the statement is made. If there is one place where there is healing... if there is one place for everybody to be... if there is one place to fill the empty spot inside of us... if there is one place that lives... if there is one place where we are really family and can reach out and touch each other...this is that place. This is that moment. When we share Christ's meal, it reaffirms those things above any other act in our lives.

"Because there is one loaf, we, who are many, are one body, for we all partake of the one loaf."

There's a second way this Sacred Moment touches us with the Grace of God. Jesus took the cup and said: "This is my blood poured out for you." The apostle that He especially loved added to that years later. John said: "...the blood of Jesus, His Son, makes us clean from all of our sin." (1 John 1:7)

His blood that makes us clean from all that is wrong in us—becomes a physical reality that we can taste—when we take that cup and drink it.

I picture me coming face-to-face with Jesus Christ. Even though the whole thought thrills me...it also makes me very uneasy. I picture me walking up to His door. He throws it open. My first instinct is to stand out on the porch because I know I don't deserve to be there.

Jesus notices my reluctance and asks me if there's something I need from Him. I explain to Him that I don't deserve to walk through that door.

He looks at me with more compassion than I know how to feel and says: "You deserve to come into my house because you are my guest."

That's just not easy for me to accept. "But, Lord, you know me. You know what a mess I am. You know how bad I've been. You know the terrible things I've done."

He just smiles at me, puts out His hand, and says: "I guess I'll just have to take your word for that. I can't seem to remember a single one." (Hebrews 8:12)

I finally make myself go in–but I just can't let go yet. "Lord", I tell Him, "I'll eat with you if you let me serve the meal."

He says: "You still don't understand. In this house to serve is the position of honor. I have earned the right to the place of honor. I do the serving here. It's like I told my brother, Peter, so many years ago: 'If you don't let me serve you–you have no part of me.' If you love me, you'll sit down and eat my meal."

With God as my witness, I will sit, I will eat, I will let Him serve me.

"Here I am!", said Jesus, "I stand at the door and knock. If anyone hears my voice and opens the door, I will eat with him, and he will eat with me."

He took the cup and said, "this now is my blood that was shed for you" ...and the blood of Jesus makes us clean.

THIRTY-NINE

WELCOME TO THE PRIESTHOOD

Understanding all of that, the sharing of Holy Communion at Serenity Church becomes a sweet, powerful, even urgent, healing moment. We are a people who are extraordinarily aware of our need for all the pieces of our puzzle that meal offers us. It is offered, given, and received every time we meet together as a Family.

In the serving and being served, the giving and receiving, of all of our Holy Moments...and specifically in the these two Holiest Moments...all of the "priests" in our Family serve together equally. So, what makes one of us a priest who can offer these sacred experiences to each other?

We believe very deeply in the principle of "the priesthood of all believers". Among other places, we're taught this by Peter. In words directed to all followers of Christ, he called each of us to stand in the gap between God and His people and exercise the priesthood of bringing those two together...

"But you are a chosen people, a royal priesthood, a holy nation, a people belonging to God, that you may declare the praises of him who called you out of darkness into his wonderful light. Once you were not a people, but now you are the people of God; once you had not received mercy, but now you have received mercy." (1 Peter 2:9-10, NIV)

We have a wide variety of ways that the Spirit enables each of us to serve His people—but ALL of us are his Royal Priests. The Spirit has created me to pastor the people that I serve. I take the responsibility of feeding the sheep that He has given me to shepherd very seriously. It's an incredible, often overwhelming privilege...with Scriptural responsibilities that can be almost crushing at times. With that said, I don't believe for a moment that my place in our Family gives me priestly privileges that are not equally shared by all the other priests in the room.

We don't have a doctrine of a separated "clergy" and "laity". We don't find that principle or those words anywhere in Scripture. The offering and receiving of our Sacred Moments...including Baptism and Holy Communion...are a privilege shared equally by all of us as Christ's priests.

We believe that whichever priest among us walked closest beside you in the journey that led you to the decision to be Baptized—should share the miracle of that moment with you physically. Our husbands baptize their wives. Our wives baptize their husbands. Mamas and daddies baptize their children. Friends baptize their friends. AA sponsors have baptized their sponsees.

I was asked by a pastor friend of mine: "Well, surely, as their pastor you're at least in the water with them, aren't you?!"

If someone asks me to share that moment with them, I'm honored and gladly accept. Otherwise, I'm not.

His follow-up question: "What's your pastoral role in that moment if you're not in the water?"

I think the sweetest, most pastoral spot of all is to be standing there waiting for them to come out of the water and hand them a dry towel. As their pastor, my most frequent role in those moments is "congregational towel-boy".

That's a position of incredible honor and I don't take it lightly. I remember another Pastor, vastly superior to me, who chose towel duty, too. (John 13:2-5)

Our Communion services are also led and served by the other priests in the room. My role? I come and receive and am blessed to be served by some of the most faithful priests I know. Christ doesn't need any one of us to "consecrate" or make that meal holy. He's always right there in the room. Making things holy is His job.

FORTY

THE MAIN THING IS THE MAIN THING

I'm not a very complicated guy. I'm not very deep. I'm not especially smart. That's not good or bad. It just is. One of my heroes when I was a child was Popeye the Sailor Man. At some point, in most of his adventures, he would announce like a battle cry: "I am what I am and that's all that I am!" That's me. I get that.

Since I will usually get lost in "complicated"–I spend my life in Scripture looking for the "bottom line" passages. If you ask me to swim too long in profound, weighty theology, I'm eventually going to drown. Tell me the point. Give me the bottom line.

Understanding that about myself, I'm always on the hunt for a "therefore", a "so that", or a colon in Scripture. Whatever follows one of those three is usually the bottom line that I need to hear. Jesus made allowances for people like me. Periodically, He would just stop and say: "Here's everything you need to know..."

My very favorite "bottom line" passage of Scripture is in Matthew 25. I mentioned earlier that I have never been a gifted scholar. School was never easy for me. A great fantasy for me would be to start a semester knowing everything that was going to be on the final exam...in advance! That way, I could spend the whole semester concentrating on just those questions that would pass me or fail me.

The only exam that will matter eternally will come from Christ when I have finished here and meet Him face-to-face. Wouldn't it be amazing to know all the questions on that test? That way, I could spend all of my time here concentrating just on those things that matter to Him. Fortunately, for a guy like me, the Teacher who will administer that exam gave me all of the questions in advance...

Matthew 25:31-40 (NIV)... "When the Son of Man comes in his glory, and all the angels with him, he will sit on his throne in heavenly glory. All the nations will be gathered before him, and he will separate the people one from another as a shepherd separates the sheep from the goats. He will put the sheep on his right and the goats on his left. Then the King will say to those on his right, 'Come, you who are blessed by my Father; take your inheritance, the kingdom prepared for you since the creation of the world. For I was hungry and you gave me something to eat, I was thirsty and you gave me something to drink, I was a stranger and you invited me in, I needed clothes and you clothed me, I was sick and you looked after me, I was in prison and you came to visit me.' Then the righteous will answer him, 'Lord, when did we see you hungry and feed you, or thirsty and give you something to drink? When did we see you a stranger and invite you in, or needing clothes and clothe you? When did we see you sick or in prison and go to visit you?' The King will reply, 'I tell you the truth, whatever you did for one of the least of these brothers of mine, you did for me.'"

I'll never forget how shocking it was to me the first time those words actually sank in. Surely, it just can't be that simple. Isn't all of that saturated in weighty theological complication? What about all of those doctrinal doo-dads that people have fought, killed, died, hated each other, refused to fellowship each other, split and divided over for 2000 years. You mean those aren't on the test? According to the Teacher who makes all of those decisions...NO!

What He wants to know is: did we take care of the hungry, the thirsty, the lonely, the naked, the sick, the imprisoned? Did we relieve the suffering around us–in His name?

To those who do, He'll have a simply response when we meet Him face-to-face: "Come, you are blessed by my Father; take your inheritance, the kingdom prepared for you since the creation of the world...whatever you did for one of the least of these brothers of mine, you did for me."

We find ourselves having to cycle back over and over and keep reminding ourselves that "the main thing is the main thing". We have to be constantly reminded that He's just not impressed with our finely tuned property, programs, and paraphernalia. Those things just aren't on the test.

He hasn't called all of us to do the same things the same way. He doesn't expect all of us to reach and care for His hurting and broken the same way.

That's a constant struggle at Serenity Church. We look around us at an explosion of churches in every direction. Aren't we supposed to be like that? Aren't we supposed to be doing all the things they're doing?

Christ was not looking for another nice, tidy, suburban, non-denominational church when He called us to do this new thing for Him. There are literally hundreds of those within minutes of us. He called us to be "an outpost for the Kingdom".

There is great good for Christ being done in most of those places. We're just not the same as them. Not better. Not worse. We're just different. Most people aren't comfortable with differentness. We want to be like everybody else. Over and over we have to stop and remind ourselves: God did not call us to do what they do the way they do it.

The mission He gave us is clear and definable: We reach out to the 12-step recovery community and introduce them to Jesus Christ as our Higher Power.

In the late '30s, as God was forming and shaping those fellowships, the 12 Steps were quickly followed by the 12 Traditions. They explained how to keep the message strong, and the relationships healthy, so that this life-saving movement could continue to move.

Tradition 5 says: "Each group has but one primary purpose—to carry its message to the one who still suffers."

That laser beam singleness of purpose has enabled a handful of desperate drunks around a kitchen table in Akron, Ohio, to multiply into millions of people in the largest, most influential, spiritual movement of the last century.

That's who we are. We have one primary purpose: to carry Christ to the many millions in those Fellowships whose Higher Power has no name.

The more we find ourselves trying to "do church" just like our neighbors–the further we'll drift from the very specific mission that He called US to.

FORTY-ONE

A WORD OF WARNING: WE'RE MESSY!

If you think you want to live your life and walk your faith among the broken and the "unchurched"...there's something you absolutely need to know going in: BROKEN PEOPLE ARE MESSY!!

By definition, these are not people with tidy, orderly lives. Their wounds are profound. Their needs are deep, real, and relentless. We describe ourselves often as "the last house on the street". We are the place to go for people who have worn out all the other places. If they can't find Christ with us—where else would they find Him? Before you start, ask yourself some hard questions...

What are you going to do when registered sex offenders (yes, this has happened repeatedly) tell you they desperately need the fellowship of your church—but their probation requires them to have strict supervision and zero contact with children?

What do you do with what seems like a small army of children who have no concept of what it is to "behave at church"—and are brought by parents with no concept of causing them to behave?

What do you do when you're ready to walk out of a borrowed space graciously opened to you by other Christians—and you see that obscene words have been scrawled on the upholstery with an indelible pen while you have been there?

What do you do when you get three frantic phone calls in one afternoon, from families at the heart of you, who have all been notified by landlords that day that they're about to be thrown out of their home? That comes right on the heels of multiple phone calls from people you love who can't afford to go pick up prescription medications that their lives depend on?

What do you do when one of the leaders of tomorrow's service calls you from jail because an old outstanding warrant unexpectedly caught up with him?

What do you do when the woman you sat beside in church Saturday night calls you to tell you she's decided to kill herself?

What do you do when...well, the list is basically endless. This ain't your mama's neighborhood church. We're really messy!

I've been referred to more than once as a "compulsive fixer". I'm not denying the allegation. Something we all have to learn quickly going in, though, is that "fixers" are drawn to this life—and we simply can't fix everything. No matter how much we'd like to. There have been times in this journey when I've honestly felt like I was drowning in a sea of human need.

Those who would shepherd deeply wounded sheep need to especially make time to back up and breathe. Regularly. If you're not capable of that, find some other way to serve Christ.

I'm typing these words at this very moment on my iPad—sitting on the porch of the guesthouse at the Monastery. Don't even ask how complicated it is to charge an iPad battery in the desert—that's a whole separate story! I didn't possibly have time right now to pull loose and be here. The truth is: I didn't have time not to.

Is there anything more important than being present right now for someone who needs you? Yes, there is. Christ understood that best of all. Over and over, we see Him surrounded by frantic, and very real need...and walking away to go recharge Himself so that He had something to give them.

Have you ever actually listened to the instructions flight attendants give before your flight takes off? It usually goes something like this:

"In the unlikely event of a sudden loss of cabin pressure, oxygen masks will drop from overhead. If you're traveling with small children, please secure your own mask first—and then assist your children."

Really?! What kind of parent is going to see to his own safety before taking care of his kids? The point is this: if you pass out, you're useless to help your child or anybody else. If you can't breathe, you can't help anybody else breathe.

Christ especially loves His broken sheep. I do, too. But understand going in: WE'RE MESSY! Often, we can't fix all of that hurt and brokeness.

FORTY-TWO

"WE CONTINUED..."

It's generally understood in my world that the first 9 Steps help us to not die. The last 3 Steps teach us how to live...

10. We continued to take personal inventory and when we were wrong promptly admitted it.

11. We sought through prayer and meditation to improve our conscious contact with God, as we understood Him, praying only for knowledge of His will for us and the power to carry that out.

12. Having had a spiritual awakening as the result of these Steps, we tried to carry this message to others, and to practice these principles in all our affairs.

Our victory over the things that destroy us is bought "one day at a time" by continuing the spiritual housekeeping, staying deeply connected to God, and helping someone else to not die... every day.

There's a lot of debate, particularly among Christians in recovery, over the "recovered" or "recovering" issue. If I truly have faith in God's ability to lift me out of this pit—isn't it showing a lack of faith to introduce myself years later as still fighting that battle? People ask me regularly: "John, you've been clean and sober for nearly 25 years now. When can you stop doing all of this and just get on with your life? Aren't you over this yet?!"

This is my answer to that question: My salvation is assured and unshakable. My recovery is not.

For me, the greatest arrogance I can imagine is to believe, even for a moment, that the Enemy knows something that works really well with me....he found something that nearly killed me and did damage to everybody and everything around me...and he forgot about it! Without question, we have supernatural help in winning our battles. That help is contingent on our continuing to fight.

Isn't that what Paul was saying about his battles? He believed that when we declare that our battle is over...we're in the greatest danger of all:

"So, if you think you are standing firm, be careful that you don't fall!" 1 Corinthians 10:12 (NIV)

"Not that I have already obtained all this, or have already been made perfect, but I press on to take hold of that for which Christ Jesus took hold of me. Brothers, I do not consider myself yet to have taken hold of it. But one thing I do: Forgetting what is behind and straining toward what is ahead, I press on toward the goal to win the prize for which God has called me heavenward in Christ Jesus." Philippians 3:12-14 (NIV)

"Brothers, if someone is caught in a sin, you who are spiritual should restore him gently. But watch yourself, or you also may be tempted. Carry each other's burdens, and in this way you will fulfill the law of Christ." Galatians 6:1-2 (NIV)

I love how The Message translates his challenge to never let up on the fight:

"I don't know about you, but I'm running hard for the finish line. I'm giving it everything I've got. No sloppy living for me! I'm staying alert and in top condition. I'm not going to get caught napping, telling everyone else all about it and then missing out myself." 1 Corinthians 9:26-27 (MSG)

So, here's my story today: "Hi, I'm John. I'm a very grateful recovering drug addict and alcoholic. By the grace of God, I'm clean and sober, one day at a time, for 9009 days today."

FORTY-THREE

STANDING ON THE SHOULDERS OF GIANTS

"We are like dwarfs on the shoulders of giants, so that we can see more than they, and things at a greater distance. Not by virtue of any sharpness of sight on our part, or any physical distinction, but because we are carried high and raised up by their giant size." Bernard of Chartres, 12th Century

In July of 2010, Kay and I went to spend some time with our daughter, son-in-law, and 2 year-old Luke. They were temporarily living in Cleveland, Ohio. We were all excitedly anticipating the arrival of our twins, MaryLee and Jack.

On our drive back home, I had planned a pilgrimage that had been deep in my heart for a long time. We pulled off the interstate in Akron and made our way downtown to the old Mayflower Hotel. What had once been the crown jewel of downtown Akron is now low-cost housing for the poor and homeless.

Standing at the grand staircase that leads down from the lobby to the street level, I could picture a frantic Bill Wilson walking down that staircase and turning right to the bar at street level. The bartender there had changed his dollar bill for a handful of nickels. I walked over to that door. It was locked, but looking through the glass I could see that it was no longer a bar. It was a big open room with folding chairs in a circle in the middle. There was a coffee pot set up in the corner. The 12 Steps and 12

Traditions were hanging on the wall. The bar of the Mayflower Hotel is now an AA hall.

We drove from there to 855 Ardmore Avenue. Dr. Bob's house. We were welcomed at the front door by a local AA member who told us the story of that surprisingly small white frame house on the corner. After Bob and Anne died, their children sold the house. It had changed hands several times and finally became a "frat house" for a nearby college. One Sunday morning, some local AA folks happened to drive by and the front yard was littered with beer cans from a party the night before. That just wasn't right. They began to raise funds and were eventually able to buy it.

They contacted Bob and Anne's children and were thrilled to find that most of the original furnishings were still intact. Their kids had put most of it in storage. It was still there. They were excited to donate what they had and helped with the restoration.

As the woman led us from room to room, she explained that this wasn't a "museum" in the classic definition. This was a home to all of us whose lives had been changed by what God had done there. She invited me to sit down at the kitchen table where that first circle of us met with Bill and Dr. Bob—frantically searching together for the solution. She led me into the little dining room where Bill had banged out the Big Book. I sat down at the table and put my hands on the keys of that old typewriter that sits there in its place like it had never been moved.

We went upstairs where there are three small bedrooms and the only bath in the house. Anne's dress is still laid out on the bed like she's going to put it on at any moment. We walked into the next room where Bill and Lois had stayed that summer that

God was giving birth to the thing that would eventually save millions of lives.

The last stop on the tour was the third bedroom. She explained that Bill and Dr. Bob always referred to that as the "Surrender Room". When someone had completed their 3rd Step they would lead them in there, kneel beside that bed, and pray together the 3rd Step prayer. She pointed to the bed. There was a Big Book opened to that prayer. She asked if I'd like to be left alone for a while. I told her I would. As she went downstairs I walked over to that spot, as so many had before me, knelt, and prayed:

"God, I offer myself to Thee—to build with me and to do with me as Thou wilt. Relieve me of the bondage of self, that I may better do Thy will. Take away my difficulties, that victory over them may bear witness to those I would help of Thy Power, Thy Love, and Thy Way of life. May I do Thy will always!"

There was still one more stop I needed to make before we left for home. We followed directions the woman at the house had given me and found an enormous old cemetery nearby. As we approached the majestic iron gates, Kay chuckled and asked: "How will we ever find one grave in the middle of all of this?" As we drove through the gates she got her answer. A large sign said: "Dr. Bob's Grave", and had a red arrow pointing to the left. Apparently we weren't the only ones with this idea!

After following several more arrows, we found what I was looking for. I walked over to the big stone over Dr. Bob's and Anne's graves. I stood there and thanked him for the way he had allowed God to use him to help save my life.

Just before we walked back to the car, I took a Serenity Church medallion out of my pocket and left it there on that stone.

I will spend the rest of my life living my gratitude for someone who walked out of that little house on Ardmore Avenue and "carried the message" to someone... who shared it with someone... who shared it with someone... who shared it with someone... who shared it with me.

God, may I always be there when the next one walks through that door and doesn't want to die.

"Therefore, since we are surrounded by such a great cloud of witnesses, let us throw off everything that hinders and the sin that so easily entangles, and let us run with perseverance the race marked out for us." Hebrews 12:1

Made in the USA
Charleston, SC
17 January 2016